AMERICAN

Foreign Service

AMERICAN

Foreign Service

J. RIVES CHILDS

WITH A FOREWORD BY JOSEPH C. GREW

KENNIKAT PRESS
Port Washington, N. Y./London

ACKNOWLEDGMENTS

From GOVERNMENT CAREER SERVICE
by Leonard Dupee White. Reprinted with
the permission of The University of Chi-
cago Press.

From SCHOOL FOR AMBASSADORS by J.
A. A. J. Jusserand. Reprinted with the
permission of G. P. Putnam's Sons.

AMERICAN FOREIGN SERVICE

Manufactured by Taylor Publishing Company   Dallas, Texas

FOREWORD

THE DECADE which lies ahead will undoubtedly be the most important in the history of the Foreign Service of the United States. There could, therefore, be no more fortunate time than now for the publication of this able analysis of the Service, and I hope that many Americans will read this book, for it presents a sound and accurate picture of the Foreign Service and its problems.

There have been two major changes in American representation abroad during this century. The first resulted from the passage in 1924 of the Rogers Act which amalgamated the old diplomatic and consular services into a single Foreign Service of the United States. In 1925 Tracy Hollingsworth Lay, Consul General of the United States, wrote his book on the Service which has been the definitive work on the subject for over twenty years. Last summer the Congress passed the Foreign Service Act of 1946 on which the Service operates today, so that we now have what is virtually a new Service, and this volume takes the place of Consul General Lay's excellent work.

The Honorable James Rives Childs, who is serving today as the American Minister to Saudi Arabia and our representative to Yemen, is a distinguished officer of the Foreign Serv-

[v]

ice. I have known Mr. Childs for many years and have respected and admired his work. He has passed through the grades of the Service, having filled the positions of Consul, Second Secretary, First Secretary, Counselor of Legation, and Consul General, and has served not only abroad but also in the Department of State. Among the posts to which he has been assigned are Jerusalem, Bucharest, Cairo, Teheran, and Tangier, his wide experience thus having given him a broad understanding of our Service and its many ramifications.

As with every government service, the two principal problems today in the Foreign Service are people and money. As long as able men such as Mr. Childs form the backbone of the Foreign Service, we shall be skillfully represented throughout the world, and I hope and believe that the Service will continue to attract some of the best of America's young men.

The effectiveness of the Service, however, and its attractiveness to the outstanding young American will both depend on the appropriations which the Congress votes for the Service. Today it is still uncertain whether the bright future foretold by the new legislation can be fully realized, for many of the reforms are still awaiting funds. I believe, however, that the interest of the American people in their foreign relations and our increasing consciousness of America's place in world affairs will provide not only the men but the money to do the job.

While I do not necessarily endorse all of Mr. Childs's opinions, it is my hope that this book will be a valuable guide to those who are interested in the technique and the problems of American representation abroad.

JOSEPH C. GREW

Washington, D. C.
March 19, 1947.

CONTENTS

[vii]

CONTENTS

AMERICAN

Foreign Service

I

THE EVOLUTION OF
THE FOREIGN SERVICE

THE NEED to deal with other nations created the Foreign Service, and it has developed in response to the urgency and complexity of those dealings. During periods, such as the present, when the attention of the nation has been turned outward and our relations with other states have been a matter of critical concern to all thoughtful citizens, the Foreign Service has been made stronger and more effective; for it has then received a greater measure of public support and drawn to itself a greater proportion of men possessing both outstanding ability and valid experience. Its evolution has, therefore, been a series of mutations, with long lapses and even regressions in between. But the development has always been in the same direction; toward a professional service made up of carefully selected, well-trained and highly disciplined public servants who spend most of their lives in the conduct of their nation's affairs abroad, and—like officers of the military service—make their careers within the organization itself.

The Foreign Service was actually established during the

War for Independence. It was clear that the outcome of the Revolution itself, and the establishment of the new nation, depended upon support from abroad. Diplomats were chosen from among the most distinguished men of the time. News of the negotiations conducted by Benjamin Franklin, John Adams, and John Jay was as anxiously awaited as word from the armies in the field, and their successes brought almost as great popular acclaim as victories in battle. Franklin, who had served for a number of years in London as representative of Pennsylvania and other States, and later was one of the three commissioners who promoted the recognition of the Republic by France, was as outstanding in experience as in ability. The Continental Congress elected him Minister Plenipotentiary to France in 1787.

The framers of the Constitution established the legal basis from which the Foreign Service grew and in which it still has its roots:

He [The President] shall have power, by and with the consent of the Senate, to make treaties, provided that two-thirds of the senators present concur; and he shall nominate, and by and with the advice and consent of the Senate, shall appoint ambassadors, other public ministers and consuls . . . and all other officers of the United States, whose appointments are not herein otherwise provided for, and which shall be established by law.

Moreover, by his constitutional executive powers and his duty to report on the state of the union, the President is made responsible for shaping our foreign policy and guiding the conduct of our foreign affairs.

Congress was quick to implement our foreign relations by creating an organization to carry out the policies laid down by the President, and execute overseas the laws affecting intercourse with other nations and Americans abroad. On July 27, 1789, an act was passed which was substantially the same as the present laws defining the functions of the Department of State. The present statute reads:

There shall be at the seat of government an executive department to be known as "the Department of State," and a Secretary of State who shall be the head thereof.
The Secretary of State shall perform such duties as shall from time to time be enjoined on or entrusted to him by the President relative to correspondences, commissions, or instructions to or with public ministers or consuls from the United States, or to negotiate with public ministers from foreign states or princes or to memorials or other applications from foreign public ministers or other foreigners, or to such other matters respecting foreign affairs as the President of the United States shall assign to the department, and he shall conduct the business of the department in such manner as the President shall direct.*

From the beginning a sharp distinction was drawn between the State Department and other departments of the government. Certain departments, such as the Treasury, were created solely for the purpose of carrying out enactments of Congress, but this was not at all true of the State Department. Hackworth points out that:

The sole purpose of that organization was to carry out, not orders, as expressed in legislation or resolution, but the will of the executive. In all cases the President could direct or control, but in the "Presidential" Department he could determine *what should be done,* as well as *how it should be done.*†

In 1790, three years after the adoption of the Constitution, Congress passed an act authorizing the President to expend not to exceed $40,000 annually for the support of such persons as he might commission to serve the United States in foreign parts. An outfit was allowed each minister to fit him for

* Code of Laws, Title V, Sections 151, 156.
† Hackworth, Digest of International Law, Volume 4, page 623.

his post but the total of his salary and outfit were not to exceed $9,000 per annum.

The first law precisely defining the powers and duties of American consular officers was passed in 1792. This initial legislation gave authority to consuls to receive marine protests and declarations from masters of vessels, to give copies under the consular seal, to settle the estates of American citizens dying within the consular district, to secure property saved from wrecks, to accept the deposit of ship's papers, and to afford relief to destitute American seamen. A supplementary act of February 28, 1803, further defined the duties of consular officers towards masters of vessels and the protection of American seamen and shipping. Even before the legislation of 1792, President Washington had appointed fifteen consular officers abroad under the authority given him by the Constitution.

During the Federal period—roughly from 1798 to 1825— the struggling Republic had one of the better foreign services in the world. It was a very small one in numbers, but its quality on the whole was high. The spoils system had not, as yet, made appointments a matter of political favoritism and men were chosen whose experience and ability made them outstanding. White in his *Government Career Service* describes the period as follows:

The original American tradition, established by the Federalists and accepted on the whole by the early Democratic-Republicans, was entirely in favor of a permanent, established, and respected public service in which careers were not only possible but were almost inevitable. Washington set our infant public service on a high standard, resolutely refusing to allow influence of any kind to creep into his appointments. John Adams maintained the high level which Washington had set. . . .

. . . Jefferson . . . fundamentally accepted the budding traditions of the public service which ruled the first twelve years of the life of the young Republic. He did insist upon the general doctrine of equality of opportunity for each of the two political groups, but subject to such equality he declared with undoubted sincerity, "I return with joy to that state of things when the only questions concerning a candidate shall be: Is he honest? Is he capable? Is he faithful to the Constitution?"

As a matter of fact, from 1789 to 1829, a substantial period of forty years, the federal service was developing along sound nonpolitical lines, unbroken by change of administration, affected no doubt by a certain amount of personal intrigue, but steadily forming a healthy tradition of permanence, integrity, and competence.

The first forty years of the Republic are, somewhat sentimentally, called the "Golden Age of American Diplomacy." The next ninety years might, with equal propriety, be called the "Dark Age." (The British consular service was organized along permanent lines in 1833, but it was not until almost a hundred years later in 1906, that the American consular service was given the semblance of a permanent foundation, according to the *Encyclopaedia Britannica*.) After the War of 1812 both our dependence upon Europe and our fear of it, waned rapidly. At the same time, the energies of the nation became absorbed in exploring, settling, and exploiting the continent. Except for a few communities along the seaboards where such industries as whaling and the China trade gave a tenuous connection with distant lands, the United States became increasingly provincial.

Representation abroad, being outside the focus of public attention, fell prey to the spoils system even more easily than did domestic offices. "In a nutshell," wrote Theodore Roosevelt, "the spoils or patronage theory is that public office is primarily designed for partisan plunder." The diplomatic and consular posts abroad became, in effect, part of the sub-

[5]

legal machinery of election. They were awarded in repayment for campaign contributions and the delivery of blocks of votes. Under such circumstances, overseas representatives of integrity and ability—such as Consul Nathaniel Hawthorne at Liverpool—were the rare exceptions.

The high diplomatic posts were usually given to generous contributors and powerful politicians who wanted to enhance their prestige and satisfy the social ambitions of their wives. The consular posts were happy hunting grounds for the avaricious. The fees went into the consul's pocket; at big ports such as Hamburg and London, the yearly plunder often exceeded the salary of the President of the United States. The less profitable consulates were usually given to lower-grade politicians and "ward heelers" whom the party in power wished to reward in some small way, or remove from the scene.

Against self-interest, reform in the national interest made slow headway. In 1833, Edward Livingston, Secretary of State under Andrew Jackson, made a set of recommendations designed to correct the abuses. But the politicians of the times prevented them from being acted upon until 1855, when Congress passed a law "to remodel the diplomatic and consular systems of the United States." The next year, this was replaced by an act which—though for a long time more honored in the breach than in the observance—shaped the development of the Foreign Service for almost a hundred years.

Besides defining the duties of consular officers more precisely, the Act of 1856 established three classes. Those of the first class were placed upon a salary basis, and prohibited from engaging in private trade. Those in the second class received salaries, but were permitted to engage in private business. Those in the third class remained on a fee basis. The merit principle was introduced into the consular service by a pro-

[6]

vision that a corps of "consular pupils" be appointed by the President when the Secretary of State had obtained evidence of their qualifications and fitness for office "by examination or otherwise."

This act also established an important administrative principle. The President was authorized "to prescribe such regulations and make and issue such orders and instructions not inconsistent with the Constitution or any law of the United States, in relation to the duties of all diplomatic and consular officers." As Mr. Tracy Lay has observed, "This provision had the effect of giving the force of law to Executive orders and other regulations of the President, in which regard it has formed the basis of all subsequent consular regulations and instructions to diplomatic officers." *

The effects of this act upon the diplomatic service were scarcely less far reaching. Ranking diplomats were for the first time provided with regular assistance, by the creation of the position of secretary of legation. The salaries of ambassadors were set at $17,500 per annum, and of ministers at $10,000. These salaries were not changed until 1946 and, though adequate when established, came to restrict and harass the Foreign Service seriously.

The improvements which might have resulted from this basic charter for the Foreign Service could only be realized through subsidiary legislation, executive order, and wise and vigorous administration within the State Department. None of these were forthcoming during the remainder of the nineteenth century. The Civil War focussed public attention upon domestic problems; during the period that followed, reconstruction and industrial development at home were far more absorbing than foreign affairs. There was little appreciation

* Lay, *Foreign Service of the United States*, page 17.

of the need for a competent diplomatic and consular service, and consequently little pressure on either the Congress or the President. O. Henry's picture of the disreputable role played by American consuls under the spoils system is not exaggerated. Consular officers, knowing that the powerful political interests which had given them their posts would sustain them no matter what they did, were ruthless in exacting tribute by whatever means came to hand. Shipowners were their particular prey, as the power of the consul over the master of a vessel in port is almost absolute. To avoid delays to which the consul might subject their vessels, shipowners and masters were compelled to pay the financial tribute imposed upon them as the extralegal price of expediting the services consular officers were required by law to perform for stated fees. Officers at particularly busy ports were able to retire in affluence after four years' tenure granted them by the administration in power.

President Cleveland, who defined public office as a public trust, endeavored to correct these abuses, but the succeeding administration reverted to the spoils system which persisted in the Foreign Service until 1906.

The Spanish-American War first brought the realization that the United States had become one of the great powers. The first stirrings of the awakening American giant were marked by a greater interest on the part of certain sections of American industry in markets abroad for their specialized products. American exports, which in the five-year period 1891–1895 had amounted to an average annual value of only $892,421,000, rose steadily and attained in the five-year period 1901–1905 an average annual value of $1,453,803,000. An increasing number of American businessmen went abroad to investigate the potential markets for their products. For the first time they encountered American consular officers directly. Many of them, seeing that the poor quality of consular officers was bad for their business, complained to the Congress and the administration. Since these businessmen commanded more votes than many of the claimants for consular posts, their influence carried correspondingly greater weight.

The result of all these factors was the first modern reform of the foreign service through an act passed in 1906. Secretary of State Elihu Root and President Theodore Roosevelt were the chief architects. This legislation dealt only with the consular service, the chief sufferer from the irregularities of the spoils system, and provided for its thorough reorganization. Consular posts were classified and graded; the prohibition against engaging in business was extended to all consular officers receiving a salary of more than $1,000. An inspection system of consulates was provided and a definite system of accounting was introduced which put an end to many irregularities which had been practiced to the detriment of the nation for almost a century.

Although the act itself did not prescribe a merit system, it made possible the application of such a system to the consular service. In June, 1906, President Roosevelt issued an Executive Order which provided that appointments to the lower grades could be made only after examination; promotion thereafter was to be based upon ability and efficiency shown in the service. In explanation of the purpose of his executive order, President Roosevelt declared:

The spoils system of making appointments to and removals from office is so wholly and unmixedly evil; is so emphatically un-American and undemocratic, and is so potent a force for degradation in our public life, that it is difficult to believe that any intelligent man of ordinary decency who has looked into the subject can be its advocate. As a matter of fact, the arguments in favor of the "merit system" and against the "spoils system" are not only convincing, but they are absolutely unanswerable.

In 1909, President Taft issued an executive order putting the appointment and promotion of diplomatic service personnel below the grades of minister and ambassador, on the same merit basis. Moreover, the order directed the Secretary of State to report to the President the names of those secretaries in the diplomatic service who had demonstrated special capacity for promotion to the ranks of chiefs of mission. Thus, more than a hundred years after the Republic was founded, career men in this branch of the Foreign Service were at last permitted the fair reward of meritorious service, and the nation was able to avail itself of the experience and ability of outstanding individuals who had spent their mature lives in the conduct of foreign affairs.

The improvements introduced by Presidents Roosevelt and Taft, for all their revolutionary character, worked better in theory than in practice. The salaries paid consular officers were generally lower than able and competent men could obtain in private walks of life; the salary range of diplomatic officers was ridiculously inadequate. The consular and diplomatic branches of the Foreign Service were quite distinct, and the highest post to which a consular officer could aspire after a lifetime of service was that of consul general. No allowances of any kind were provided either diplomatic or consular officers. As the average expenditures of a diplomatic secretary were from $5,000 to $12,000 for his living expenses alone, and his maximum salary was $3,000 a year, this service was entirely closed until 1924 to any American not possessing a substantial private income. The result was that the diplomatic service continued until 1924 to be the almost exclusive preserve of the sons (and sons-in-law) of America's rich families, attracted to diplomatic service abroad for the social prestige it gave them. Not all of these officers were indifferent to the serious tasks of diplomacy; some of them proved to be among the most distinguished of our career service. But far too many were dilettantes. The way in which such men served their country is perfectly illustrated by a telegram received by the State Department from Ambassador Hammond, then Chief of our Mission in Spain. "I have urgent need of the services of a polo-playing diplomatic secretary." It is small wonder that the legend of "white-spatted," "cookie-pushing" officers attached itself to the American Foreign Service. This was the kind of officer which the nation, in effect, asked for by closing the service to men who had to work for a living. As always, the United States got just about what it was willing to pay for.

By 1915, with the outbreak of war and the increasing need felt for a stronger Foreign Service, it was found that the existing legislation of 1906 cast the consular service in too rigid and inflexible a form. The Act of February 5, 1915 made the service more flexible and its officers easier to deploy as circumstances required. Moreover, this act introduced for the first time in statutory form, the merit principle in both the consular and diplomatic services.

The end of the First World War found the United States a dominant world power. Responsibilities in the field of foreign affairs had drastically increased. It was obvious that the type of Foreign Service which then existed was entirely inadequate to the task at hand. Secretary of State Robert Lansing urged upon Congress "remedial and constructive legislation."

The result was the Act of May 24, 1924, commonly known as the "Rogers Act," after Congressman John Jacob Rogers of Massachusetts, the "Father of the Modern American Foreign

Service." This act combined the diplomatic and consular services, and officially gave the title Foreign Service Officer to members of both branches of the service. It provided for appointment by open, competitive examination with promotion strictly on a merit basis; established a new salary and retirement scale and gave authority for a system of representation allowances. In brief, it placed our Foreign Service for the first time upon a sound professional basis.

The economic situation in the United States, however, curtailed the immediate improvement that had been anticipated from the Rogers Act. During the years from 1924 to 1929 the returns in business, financially speaking, were far greater than the rewards offered by the Foreign Service. The public support of disarmament made a future in the armed forces appear bleak, and a number of able men from the Army and Navy transferred to the Foreign Service. A number of other outstanding men entered, at the time, because of a keen interest in the work ahead for the Service and the feeling that the promise of a worthwhile career in the field of foreign affairs had, at last, been opened up. But on the whole, it remained difficult during the 1924–1929 boom period to attract to the Foreign Service the necessary number of candidates of outstanding caliber.

The crash of 1929–1930 changed the entire picture. The new Service by then had five years behind it. It seemed secure from political storms. The dismal era of the early 1930's, with business jobs scarce and often unattractive, for the first time made government careers in an organization like the Foreign Service attractive to the young college graduate. Franklin D. Roosevelt reinforced the interest of the young people of America in government as a career. The New Deal brought to Washington a host of aspiring youth seeking a chance to help mold America's future. Thus during the decade of the

1930's the Foreign Service experienced little difficulty in attracting high-caliber candidates.

Until 1927 the Foreign Service, directed and supervised by the Department of State had been the sole Foreign Service of our government and represented in foreign parts all the federal departments. The Rogers Act of 1924 had stated that "Hereafter the diplomatic and consular services of the United States shall be known as the *Foreign Service of the United States.*" Between 1927 and 1935, three additional American foreign services were established. All four operated abroad until 1939, to the confusion of foreigners and the frequent despair of Americans.

In the boom period of 1924–1929 American exports had expanded enormously. The fledgling Foreign Service of the Rogers Act was too new and too handicapped by inadequate home direction to be able to give the extensive services demanded by American exporters who were opening up world markets on the proceeds of American loans. Herbert Hoover, as Secretary of Commerce, was therefore able to persuade Congress, in 1927, to form a separate foreign commerce service. Under Mr. Hoover's direction this service was built up into an efficient organization which operated on behalf of American business to promote American exports. But, the efficiency of this service could not be maintained in the face of the great crash of 1929 and the shrinking of world trade. Political patronage crept into its appointments; morale began to sag and the work of the commerce service suffered in consequence.

This occurred at a time when exactly the opposite was happening in the Foreign Service supervised and directed by the State Department. The Moses-Linthicum Act, passed in 1931, made definite improvements in compensation, through the establishment of various allowances; the entrance requirements were exacting; a far higher caliber of candidate sought entry than ever before. Patronage found no chink to enter and the Service was encouraged by an increasing proportion of career men appointed as ministers and ambassadors.

In 1930, following the example of the Department of Commerce, the Department of Agriculture persuaded Congress to establish, on a somewhat smaller scale, a foreign agricultural service. The foreign service of the Department of Agriculture comprised a small but very able group of agricultural specialists who were attached to our embassies and legations abroad. Besides endeavoring to promote the sale of surplus American farm products, they filled efficiently a specialized field of reporting on such subjects as agricultural market prospects.

The Bureau of Mines (of the Department of the Interior) was the next agency of the government to receive statutory authority, by legislation passed in 1935, to send its own representatives to foreign countries. This foreign service of the Department of the Interior sent a few mineral specialists from time to time to the foreign field.

In addition to these four statutory services, other Departments and agencies sent temporary representatives abroad. These representatives frequently maintained little or no connection with the other American foreign service establishments.

Conflict and confusion were inevitable—for the State Department had already been given authority by law to perform the services rendered by these foreign representatives of other departments. That is, the Foreign Service as an arm of the State Department had already been given responsibility for all types of reporting and trade promotion abroad. Moreover, the State Department must receive through the Foreign Service complete reports on *all phases* of the life of nations with which we deal, in order to carry out its responsibilities toward

[14]

the planning and execution of a well-integrated set of foreign policies adapted to the needs of the times.

The separate Agriculture, Commerce, and Interior services, however, reported directly to their respective departments, and it was never possible to achieve adequate co-ordination of the work of the four services in the field. As a result there was much duplication of effort, waste of public funds, and at times rather bitter rivalry, which may have amused the foreign observer, but no American. The foreign government officials, on their part, were confused by our multiplicity of foreign representation.

By the late 1930's the situation clearly required remedial action. Under President Roosevelt's direction a study was made to find out how the federal establishments could be reduced in number, regrouped, and their functions reallocated. A reorganization act was passed in 1939. The principle of unity of representation abroad by a single organization which served the government as a whole—the principle laid down in the Rogers Act of 1924—was reinstated and the foreign services of the Departments of Commerce and Agriculture were merged into the Foreign Service of the United States under the direction and supervision of the Department of State. The few mineral specialists abroad in behalf of the Bureau of Mines were consolidated into the Foreign Service in 1943. The foreign service of the Treasury Department still remains, however, as a separate unity.

In 1945 the United States emerged from war into a timorous new world; a world harrowed by the knowledge that a paranoid nation could bring disaster to all, and overshadowed by the atomic explosives we ourselves devised. The situation which created the "Golden Age of American Diplomacy" had been almost completely reversed. Then, our own weakness made diplomacy a principal arm of national defense. After the Second World War our very strength thrust international leadership upon us, placing in our hands the lives of millions overseas. Moreover, there is no longer any ultimate salvation in national defense. We are on guard, not against defeat or conquest, but against total destruction. World balance and world security are the last hope, and we cannot escape our responsibility for their authorship. The full cycle of change thus made the need for an effective Foreign Service even more critical than in the first precarious days of independence.

By the war's end, the accumulated changes of the past quarter century had suddenly burst the bounds of tradition and revolutionized intercourse between nations. Whereas the contact between peoples was once remote and at a few points only—government official dealing with official, banker with banker, trader with trader, and social leader with social leader —nations now live side by side, exchanging goods and services, ideas and technology, like rural neighbors trading horses. And, like neighbors, bickering continually. The international mutual-help organizations which sprang up to deal with the problems of a world shrunk to county size in space time and prodigiously increased in complexity, numbered into the dozens.

To cope with its responsibilities under the changed conditions of international intercourse, the United States had a Foreign Service woefully handicapped by a poor administrative foundation in law.

It was like an antique house which has been added to, generation after generation, as the family fortunes waxed and waned and new members were continually added; a house agreeable because of its age and traditions, but without architecture and totally unsuited to modern living.

The State Department determined that, for the first time since the founding of the Republic, the Foreign Service would be designed for the future instead of the past. The Foreign Service itself—in collaboration with experts in many fields and members of Congress—planned a new organizational and administrative structure. This plan was embodied in "An Act to improve, strengthen and expand the Foreign Service of the United States and to consolidate and revise the laws relating to its administration." * Known as "The Foreign Service Act of 1946," it was approved in August of that year and went into effect in November.

* Titles I through X of this act are republished without abridgment as Appendix A.

II

THE FOREIGN SERVICE
AS A CAREER

IN 1946 the Foreign Service maintained some three hundred establishments abroad; it must steadily increase their number even after the deficit caused by the Second World War is made up, if for no other reason than that the increase in world population will extend foreign relations into new areas. These establishments range all the way from embassies staffed by three hundred or more, to minor consulates manned by a scant handful.

Embassies are maintained in the most important capitals of the world, and in each capital in Latin America. They are headed by *ambassadors,* whose full official title is "Ambassador Extraordinary and Plenipotentiary." Ambassadors are accredited to chiefs of state and "represent in their persons the President"; because of this unusual status, they enjoy special consideration in the countries of their assignment.

Legations are maintained in the capitals of other countries. Legations are headed by *ministers.* Their full title is "Envoy Extraordinary and Minister Plenipotentiary." A minister is accredited to the chief of state, but does not represent the person of the President. In practice, there is not a great deal of difference between a minister and an ambassador.

Consulates General are maintained in important commercial cities, and *consulates* in lesser communities. The former are headed by *consuls general,* the latter by *consuls* or *vice-consuls.* In capital cities, the consulate general or consulate is usually part of the embassy or legation. A consular officer is granted what is known as an *exequatur,* which entitles him to exercise his functions, by the government of the country in which he is stationed. He has no representative character. He deals—not with the high officials of the national government in the country of his assignment—but with local authorities, such as governors, prefects, mayors, and chiefs of police.

Missions are diplomatic establishments of the United States, and have authority over the consular establishments in a designated area. (For example, the establishments in British colonies are consular and under the diplomatic mission to the governing country.) A *chief of mission* is any person who is appointed by the President, by and with the advice and consent of the Senate, to be in charge of a diplomatic establishment, or any person assigned to be minister, chargé d'affaires, diplomatic agent or commissioner. (In a few countries which have not yet attained full self-government, there are diplomatic missions with a special status which may be under a Personal Representative of the President, or a Commissioner.) The term *chargé d'affaires* is not synonymous with the term *chargé d'affaires ad interim,* which is applied to an officer temporarily in charge of a diplomatic mission in the absence of the chief of mission.

Diplomatic missions are staffed by Foreign Service officers ranging in rank from *career minister* down through *counselor* and *first, second,* and *third secretary.* Officers performing some types of specialized work are known as *attachés*. Consular establishments and sections are staffed by officers holding ranks ranging from *consul general* to *vice-consul*. However, there is no distinction (except in the case of members of the Foreign Service staff branch, to be discussed later) between the diplomatic and consular services; officers are interchangeable from one type of service to the other, and may be given double titles, one consular and one diplomatic.

The knowledge required of the staff of a large mission is comparable to that possessed by the faculty of a college. Every aspect of the country's life—from food customs to territorial ambitions—must be understood thoroughly. And all that is known must be interpreted in the light of world conditions and world organization. The relations of every event to trends in international affairs, and to both international law and the laws of the United States must be considered. Most especially the interests, objectives, and policies of the United States must be used as a screen against which to evaluate every piece of information that comes in the Foreign Service officer's way, and every problem that arises. The Service thus requires officers drawn from the top stratum of the hierarchy of intelligence. It needs America's most able learners.

The Foreign Service officer lives under the spotlight of foreign public attention. The foreigners whom he meets draw their conclusions concerning the United States and its citizens, not only from what he tells them, but from the way he behaves and the kind of person he seems to be. To represent the United States fittingly, the Foreign Service officer must, therefore, be a representative of American culture and traditions at their best.

He should be a person of broad cultivation and catholic tastes, and he should possess in the highest degree the gift of getting along with people. He must be able to adapt to almost any social situation.

Moreover, the Foreign Service officer must apply his knowledge and use his social talents in practical, operating circumstances. His virtues as a scholar and a mixer are not their own reward; he has to produce results that serve his country well. Consequently, experience has a very high value in the Service. Foreign affairs are not like any of the fields of activity in which a people ordinarily gain their livelihoods; they are external to one's native land, and thus outside ordinary experience; and they must be conducted with foreigners. A good officer's skill and usefulness increase enormously with his years in the Service. Moreover, the Foreign Service officer's work requires self-discipline and devotion to take the place of the rules of work which keep most employed people steady in their jobs. He may spend the morning sweating out a report, and spend the afternoon—say—in the garden at Groppi's in Cairo, soaking up information about Egypt along with cup after cup of tea he drinks to keep pace with his knowledgeable but thirsty companion.

Mr. DeWitt C. Poole, a distinguished former Foreign Service officer, has observed: "An officer who is regularly at his desk at 9 or earlier and stays until 5 or after and turns in a visually impressive score on the quarterly work sheet, is probably earning his salary. But it is not excluded that some more studious and imaginative colleague, whose days flow less evenly, has attained a more knowing touch with the local life and people. When some situation is moving up under the horizon, the latter will likely first detect its looming and apprehend its meaning, thereby earning his salary a hundred times over at a single stroke."

One of the ablest economic counselors in the Service said, in an analysis of economic reporting: "It demands of each reporting officer a firsthand knowledge whereof he speaks. This can come only from breaking away from his desk and getting into the field at frequent intervals. A lump of coal must become something that has been handled, and not just a statistical fraction of a metric ton. There must also be imagination, the exercise of critical judgment, and a willingness to go out on a limb by making a prediction when a prediction is called for."

In short, a Foreign Service officer has to work his hardest in situations which offer every temptation to play. He has to observe as carefully as a field naturalist where other Americans are enjoying themselves in relaxed sight-seeing. He has to improvise a great many of his most useful activities, and he has to give his best to them though there is no one to see whether he is negligent or not.

He cannot, therefore, be either a dilettante or a bureaucrat. The characteristics necessary in an officer—ability to learn, comportment in keeping with his situation, skill in dealing with people, and the imagination and self-discipline to take initiative—the sum of these is professional competence, different only in particulars from that of the physician or jurist.

The United States Foreign Service is, therefore, a *professional* organization. Aside from the discipline he imposes on himself, the Foreign Service officer is subject to the discipline of his organization. He must submit with no show of insubordination to transfer, even though he is sent on very short notice to a most unpleasant spot. His job is to report, and to execute laws and policies—not to create policy or expound his own views. His actions are, therefore, not free, but controlled from above in much the same way as are those of a military officer. Very probably, General Eisenhower's principle that the most valuable quality that an Army officer can have, is *selflessness*, applies equally to Foreign Service officers. They must hold the Service itself in higher regard than their own opinions or their own interests.

To almost every Foreign Service officer there comes a time, also, when he must think of the Service first and his own person second. That hour came for Paul Knabenshue, Minister to Bagdad, in the summer of 1941 when Rashid Ali led a rebellion against the party favoring the Allies. For more than a month, the Minister, his staff, and almost two hundred American, British, and other nationals withstood siege in the legation. Mr. Knabenshue died shortly afterward of a small infection incurred under the dangerous conditions which prevailed.

Disease is probably the most serious hazard faced by the Foreign Service, though officers have often risked—and sometimes met—violent death in line of duty. Very few are lucky enough to escape dangerous posts throughout their entire service, and the working life of many has been shortened by such diseases as amoebic dysentery and malaria. These hazards are accepted as an inevitable part of an officer's duties—as combat assignments are accepted in the Army.

For these reasons, the Foreign Service is a *career* service. Those who enter it expect to live in it and accept its discipline throughout their working years.

If Americans capable of becoming professionals in the conduct of foreign affairs are to commit themselves to a career service, the Foreign Service itself must be a fit place for them. It was made so by the Act of 1946, mentioned at the close of the preceding chapter. This act provided for (1) a promotion system which encourages the individual officer to improve his competence steadily; (2) compensation and allowances which make the financial rewards attractive in comparison to professional work outside government service; (3) retirement benefits, health provisions, and other measures which insure adequate security to the Foreign Service officer and his family; (4) recruitment on the basis of special aptitude for the work; (5) a system of in-service education, by both academic work and especially arranged experience. In addition, the Foreign Service is now able to recruit specialists to perform functions lying somewhat outside the scope of regular diplomatic and consular officers.

If a system is to induce men to give their best and grow in competence, there has to be room at the top—and room to get to the top. Promotion, therefore, has to be co-ordinated with separation. In the Foreign Service, room is made at the top by retiring career ministers at age 65, and the Class 1 officers at 60. Room is made on the promotion ladder by retiring all officers who are not promoted.

There are six classes below the rank of career minister. Each year that an officer stays in a particular class, he receives an in-grade increase in salary. But he can only stay in each class a given number of years. The length of time an officer may remain in each class is set by administrative regulation. An officer who fails to achieve promotion, has reached the ceiling of his development. He is not suitable timber for the top positions of ambassador and minister, and it is to the best interests of the Service to replace him with a man—equally competent in the work of a subordinate—who may develop further. The procedure is very much like the United States Navy's "promotion-up or selection-out" system.

Promotions are made by carefully chosen boards which base their judgments on the best obtainable evidence of value to the Service. "Best obtainable evidence," means efficiency records scientifically designed and scientifically validated. The Foreign Service employs the methods which modern personnel psychology has provided for objectively measuring individual performance against actual, on-the-job criteria of success. The promotion system is as free from favoritism, guesswork, and prejudice as it is possible to make it.

The co-ordinated promotion and retirement procedures make it possible for a young officer to enter the service in Class 6 at a salary of $3,300, and reach Class 1 at a salary of $12,000 fifteen years later. The average time it takes to climb from Class 6 to Class 1, is twenty-seven years. How fast and how far an officer goes depends upon his merit and his growth.

The very highest positions in diplomacy are freely open to officers of the career service. Outstanding officers in Class 1 are promoted to the grade of career minister (salary of $13,500), when they are appointed ambassadors, ministers, or counselors at the more important posts, or consuls general at posts such as Shanghai or Jerusalem, or to certain high positions in the Department. If the officer ceases to serve in one of these capacities, he remains in the class of career minister, and is available for assignment to any important post in the Service or in the State Department. The most successful career ministers are appointed to ambassadorships at outstanding posts, such as Paris, and receive during service there the full salary allotted to the mission.

In the regulations governing appointments to the ranking positions, the Foreign Service Act of 1946 made one of its most important contributions to American diplomacy in general and the morale of the Service in particular. In the darkest period of the reign of the spoils system, most important posts were given as rewards for political favors; others were given to prominent men who might be—but very often were not—experienced in foreign affairs. The choice of ambassadors was seriously restricted by the fact that a man could not afford to take an important post unless he (or his wife) was wealthy; salaries had been set in 1855, and allowances for representation and maintenance of missions were inadequate. The merit principle made headway ·only gradually, and though more than half of the country's ministers and ambassadors were career officers by the end of the Second World War, it was still quite possible for a man to obtain such a post simply because he could afford it and had influence in the right places. The results were, to use an understatement, unfortunate.

For one thing, inexperienced diplomats were usually capable of performing only the ceremonial work of representation; they went to the receptions and attended the conferences—and left their subordinates to carry the burden of the work. Some of the men appointed through political influence were not even fit for representation.

Some years ago a President sent as Minister to Persia, a Southwestern politician whose name was written large in the frontier annals of his state. When he first arrived he went a number of times to gatherings in the home of an influential and cultured Englishwoman. But after a few months, these invitations abruptly ceased. Discussing the situation with a friend, the English hostess agreed that the minister was, indeed, a colorful personality; she regretted not being able to invite him, but his aim was so bad when he spit tobacco juice that he was rapidly ruining her lovely Persian carpets and she did not think his company worth the sacrifice.

These legendary personalities did not all serve long ago. It is only a few years since the chief of mission at a Latin American post made a practice of walking around the house naked, continually trailed by a native girl bearing a tray of Scotch whisky, soda, and ice.

Inexperienced diplomats hampered their staffs simply because they did not understand how the work must be done. And they often made serious trouble because, lacking sufficient discipline and devotion to the service, they did not subordinate their own opinions and ambitions to the policies laid down by the President and the Department of State.

The Service suffered internal damage because of such appointments. There was no certainty that ability, initiative, and devotion would be rewarded by one of the top posts; bitter experience engendered a feeling that the fruits cultivated by officers in subordinate positions would be plucked by the wealthy and powerful. Under such circumstances some able men were stultified by the Service; others resigned to enter more promising careers. Moreover, the uncertainty of advancment to positions in which their full capacities would be used and rewarded, caused many able men to refuse to enter the Service at all. The cumulated result was that American diplomacy always lacked experienced men of sufficient capacity to fill the higher positions capably.

It is now virtually certain that every Foreign Service officer will advance to the limit of his capabilities, if he has the will to do so. The money for maintaining a mission can come from public, rather than private funds, under the more generous system of allowances. Salaries are commensurate with those received by executives in business: chiefs of mission at Class I posts (such as London) receive $25,000 per annum; at Class II posts (such as The Hague) $20,000; at Class III posts (such as Cairo) $17,500; at Class IV posts (such as Managua) $15,000. Moreover, the Service itself has become a proving ground and a practical school for diplomats. Men highly qualified by special experience outside the Foreign Service (such as that which General Marshall gained during a varied military career crowned by service as Chief of Staff during the Second World War) are rare. It is greatly to the nation's advantage that the Foreign Service "graduates" a number of fully qualified diplomats each year.

The ranking positions of diplomacy are *political* in that the diplomat represents his State in its dealings with others. He must, therefore, be capable of synthesizing the various elements—legal, cultural, economic, and psychological—of which political situations consist. He must be skilled in all four of the "technical" phases of diplomacy—representation, reporting, negotiation, and protection of American interests. Though he may become a specialist in dealing with countries which are related in culture, language, or geography—his usefulness will be limited if he becomes principally a subject-matter specialist, or overdevelops any particular skill to the detriment of others. Foreign Service officers, therefore, get all-around experience to prepare them for the responsible post of diplomacy.

Nevertheless, much of the work of our missions requires specialists, and up until 1946 the Service was handicapped because it had no regularly established way of employing them. The Act of 1946 created the Foreign Service Reserve, to which belong officers who perform specialized functions and are not being groomed for the highest diplomatic positions. These men, drawn both from the Government and the civilian community, serve up to a maximum of four years. They include such men as information specialists, telecommunications experts, aviation authorities, petroleum specialists, and cultural attachés. Upon the termination of their assignments, they revert to inactive status and go back to their previous careers. However, men who acquire a lasting interest in the Service and who are qualified for it, may be appointed Foreign Service officers after 4 years in the Reserve, (3 years if over 31). Their salaries, positions, and titles match those of regular Foreign Service officers, and they are appointed to classes commensurate with their professional competence.

The Act of 1946 also established the Staff branch of the

Foreign Service. This consists of all Americans in the Service who are not Foreign Service officers or Reserve officers. The salary range is up to $10,000. An officer or employee of the Staff branch may be transferred to the Foreign Service officer branch after 4 years (3 years if over 31) provïded he is qualified and passes an examination.

In its upper and middle ranks the Staff branch comprises chiefly functional and administrative specialists (for example, a petroleum expert or the chief administrative officer at London, or a civil air attaché, or the disbursing officer at Paris), and lower down the junior administrative personnel, couriers, radio operators, clerks, stenographers, typists, translators, interpreters, communications personnel, commissary officers, despatch agents, code technicians, et cetera. Where appropriate, the titles of consul as well as that of vice-consul are provided for personnel of the Staff branch. This does not mean that the gulf which at one time separated the consular from the diplomatic service has yawned again. The Service takes precautions to eliminate discrimination between the Staff and Foreign Service officer branches.

It has sometimes been urged that there should be no differentiation among Foreign Service personnel and that everybody should be a Foreign Service officer. The reason for having two arms of the Service lies in the necessity of having provision for selecting and training personnel for positions of leadership and the exercise of command. The selection, promotion, and retirement system of the officer branch are designed to this end. However, to recruit and maintain the whole Service on this basis would be unnecessary and uneconomical, if not downright impossible.

The Foreign Service provides security both for officers who serve until the retirement age, and for those "selected out." Officers who are separated when in Class 2 or 3, are eligible for annuities. Those separated from Class 4 or 5 receive lump sums. Those who retire because of age or disability receive annuities. The Service also provides rent and cost-of-living allowances to enable officers to perform their work with maximum efficiency. Separation allowances are granted when health hazards make it unwise for an officer to maintain his family at his post. Travel and other service-created expenses (for example, new outfits of clothing required by transfer to a radically different climate), hospitalization, and medical care, are paid by the Government.

In order that officers will not—as in times past—have to bear the expense of representing the United States, there are authorized both representation allowances and funds for the maintenance of the establishment of the chief of mission. The latter are "allowances to the post"; they amount to $3,000 to $4,000 a year at small posts, such as Kabul, and range upward to $25,000 at such large and expensive posts as Buenos Aires, Paris, and London. Although the "post" allowance has been authorized, Congress has not yet appropriated funds for its payment. It is hoped that within the year these funds will be made available.

The Foreign Service has selected its recruits with extreme care since 1924. The professional nature of the work would, alone, make it very important to select recruits on merit. The fact that Foreign Service officers are entering upon careers comparable to those of Army and Navy officers, and receive Presidential appointments "by and with the consent of the Senate," which qualify them as eventual ministers and ambassadors, makes impartial and painstaking selection a critical necessity. The Foreign Service Act of 1946 (Sec. 516) provides that:

No person shall be eligible for appointment as a Foreign Service officer of Class 6 unless he has passed such written, oral, physical, and other examinations as the Board of Examiners for the Foreign Service may prescribe to determine his fitness and aptitude for the work of the Service, and has demonstrated his loyalty to the Government of the United States and his attachment to the principles of the Constitution. The Secretary shall furnish the President with names of those persons who have passed such examinations and are eligible for appointment as Foreign Service officers of Class 6.

The Board of Examiners of the Foreign Service, under regulations prescribed by the Secretary of State, provides for and supervises the conduct of these examinations, which before the last war were held semiannually. The Board of Examiners has played an important role in the development of the Service in insuring the selection on the basis of competitive examinations of the best qualified candidates for appointment. Not more than half of the members of this Board may be Foreign Service officers. In November 1946, the Board consisted of the Assistant Secretary of State for the administration of the Department, the Director General of the Foreign Service (who acts as Chairman in the absence of the Assistant Secretary), the Chief of the Division of Foreign Service Personnel, the Executive Director of the Board of Examiners for the Foreign Service, an officer of the Department of Commerce designated by the Secretary of Commerce and acceptable to the Secretary of State, an officer of the Department of Agriculture designated by the Secretary of Agriculture and acceptable to the Secretary of State, and the Assistant Chief Examiner of the Civil Service Commission. (In order to permit the appointment to the Service of particularly well-qualified individuals into the higher classes, which is necessary to provide the requisite elasticity, provision is made for the appointment of qualified persons as Foreign Service officers of Classes 1 to 5, inclusive. Such persons must have had prior service in the Department of State or in the Foreign Service so that there will be a record of their performance available, and they must have passed prescribed examinations.) The examinations are not the whole of the system for selecting recruits. Officers in Class 6 are on probation; the Secretary may terminate their services at any time. New officers are thus sorted out, and either promoted, or separated according to their efficiency records—which, as before noted, are scientifically validated instruments for measuring value to the service. Under some circumstances, as many as one in six Class 6 officers may be separated during their probationary period.

It is thus impossible to insure a career in the Foreign Service by "studying for the examinations." The best preparation is to be had in the better American undergraduate colleges; the social sciences, history, and languages are the most pertinent studies. The Foreign Service maintains effective liaison with institutions of higher learning, and curricula at some colleges and universities are co-ordinated with the knowledge requirements of officers.

Once a candidate has entered its ranks, the Service takes his education in charge. Its own establishment for in-service training—the Foreign Service Institute—gives him a brief orientation course. He is assigned to a mission to gain some firsthand experience, then brought back to Washington for further study at the institute and work in the State Department which gives him an understanding of that complex organization and its relationships with the missions abroad.

Throughout his career, a Foreign Service officer is given, whenever possible, assignments calculated to develop in him the breadth of knowledge and the special skills which will be demanded as he goes higher in the service. The objective is to develop diplomats through calculated experience. The more formal side of the officers' education is co-ordinated with these maturing assignments.

[3 2]

The Foreign Service Institute is a graduate institution which trains not only officers of the Service, but employees of other Government agencies for which the State Department performs functions abroad. Its staff consists of selected officers of the Foreign Service and Department of State; other Government departments; and educators and scholars from universities throughout the United States. It provides special training in languages, economic reporting, area problems, and all other important phases of foreign service in which superior and appropriate instruction is not available at other institutions.

Foreign Service officers are assigned to the Institute as their general development and special assignments require. For example, when an officer is transferred to a new post where the language, the people and their history are entirely outside his previous experience, he is (if possible) brought back to the Institute for a period of perhaps 4 months for intensive language study, general orientation and consultation. Officers who need specialized training are assigned for the requisite time for training in the appropriate field. In some specialized subjects, better training is to be had at other places, such as universities; research centers; trade, labor, agricultural, and scientific associations; or commercial firms. Officers who need the training best obtained in these places, are assigned to them for the required time.

Assignment to the Foreign Service Institute and other places of learning is an important part of the Service's policy of "re-Americanization." Experience has clearly shown that Foreign Service personnel should come to the United States as often as possible to renew their knowledge of developments at home and their feeling for the American way of life. Home leave every two years is authorized, and officers must spend at least three out of their first fifteen years of service on assignment in the United States, in addition to periods of leave of absence.

During their service in the United States officers may be assigned to the Department of State—both to provide them with experience and because they are needed there, as subsequent chapters will show. They are often assigned to other Government agencies for periods ranging up to four years. They may be assigned to temporary service to or in co-operation with the government of another country. And they may be assigned for duty "with domestic or international trade, labor, agricultural, scientific, or other conferences, congresses, or gatherings, including those whose place of meeting is in the continental United States; or for other special duties."

The Foreign Service is thus able to provide professional, highly trained men to serve with such organizations as the United Nations and its many affiliated bodies and special committees.

III

THE FOREIGN SERVICE
AND THE DEPARTMENT
OF STATE

THE MAIN JOB of the State Department is to help the President frame foreign policy, devise appropriate action for carrying it out, and take such action as has been decided upon. Presidents carry such a tremendous load that a great deal of the work of policy formation and decision as well as execution is delegated to the Secretary of State, his two Under Secretaries, his Counselor and his Assistant Secretaries, whose number varies with circumstances and the administrative theories in vogue. They in turn delegate their more detailed and less weighty responsibilities to subordinates.

The millstream that turns the intricately meshed wheels of the State Department is the flow of reports coming in from Foreign Service officers all over the world. These are the raw materials of policy. And they bring to attention the situations and events that call for executive action. Thus the reports sent in from missions abroad eventuate in the instructions, policy guides, messages for delivery to foreign governments, and other advices which set the Foreign Service officer himself in motion.

Naturally, foreign representatives sent here by other governments and acting in their behalf also influence American decisions and require action on our part. However, this phase of the State Department's work is neither so far-flung, so complex, nor so many-sided as the activities directly involving reports from overseas. Fewer people are required to do it; and it lies principally outside the scope of the Foreign Service.

Administrative reports go to the various sections of the home office of the Foreign Service itself. Most of the reports relating to foreign policy go through the seventeen *divisions* which are responsible for particular geographical areas (see accompanying chart). These divisions are further broken down into sections—called *desks*—assigned to handle relations with States and other logical units within the divisional area; for example the Division of Near Eastern Affairs has, among others, desks for Palestine, the Arabian Peninsula, and Turkey. These desk sections are under the jurisdiction of men who have had some previous experience with the country for whose affairs they are responsible, or with the general area in which it is located; they are usually Foreign Service officers. They have the initial responsibility for handling all questions—political, economic, or administrative—relating to their particular patches of earth.

The "geographical" departments are grouped into four *offices*, each in charge of a section of the globe; the offices of European Affairs, Far Eastern Affairs, and Near Eastern and African Affairs, are under one Assistant Secretary; the Office of American Republic Affairs is under another.

The Department has defined the role of the geographic Offices as follows:

The geographic Offices shall be responsible for the formulation of over-all United States policy toward the countries within their

CHART OF THE STATE DEPARTMENT'S "GEOGRAPHIC" OFFICES
(Spring, 1946)

OFFICES	DIVISIONS	COUNTRIES
European Affairs	British Commonwealth Affairs	British Commonwealth and possessions, except India, Burma, Ceylon, and possessions in Africa
	Eastern European Affairs	U.S.S.R., Poland
	Central European Affairs	Germany, Austria, Czechoslovakia
	Southern European Affairs	Albania, Bulgaria, Hungary, Italy, Rumania, San Marino, Yugoslavia, Vatican
	Northern European Affairs	Denmark, Finland, Iceland, Netherlands, Norway, Sweden, and territories of those countries.
	Western European Affairs	Andorra, Belgium, France, Liechtenstein, Luxembourg, Monaco, Portugal, Spain, Switzerland, and territories of those countries.
Far Eastern Affairs	Chinese Affairs	China
	Japanese Affairs	Japan
	Southeast Asia Affairs	Siam, Indo-China, Burma, Malaya, British North Borneo, North East Indies, Portuguese Timor, British and French island possessions in the Pacific.
	Philippine Affairs	Philippine Islands
Near Eastern and African Affairs	Near Eastern Affairs	Egypt, Greece, Iraq, Lebanon, Palestine, Trans-Jordan, Saudi Arabia, Arabian Peninsula, Syria, Turkey
	Middle Eastern Affairs	Afghanistan, Burma, Ceylon, India, Iran
	African Affairs	Ethiopia, Liberia and all other territories in Africa except Algeria and South Africa
American Republic Affairs	Mexican Affairs	Mexico
	Caribbean and Central American Affairs	Costa Rica, Cuba, Dominican Republic, El Salvador, Guatemala, Haiti, Honduras, Nicaragua, Panama
	Brazilian Affairs	Brazil
	River Plate Affairs	Argentina, Paraguay, Uruguay, Colombia, Ecuador
	North and West Coast Affairs	Bolivia, Chile, Peru, Venezuela

[37]

jurisdiction and for the co-ordination, as to these countries, of the programs and activities of other Offices and Divisions of the Department, and of other federal agencies, with over-all United States policy.

In order to form a clearer appreciation of the relation of the geographic Divisions to the field, let us consider a case which actually occurred several years ago. Italian planes bombed an American missionary outpost situated in Egyptian territory near the Ethiopian border. The Legation at Cairo telegraphed fragmentary facts concerning the incident to the Department. The telegram was routed to a Foreign Service officer dealing with Egyptian affairs. His information was supplemented by newspaper clippings and by ticker-tape reports of the news agencies, routed to him daily as a part of the Department's regular procedure for keeping its officers informed.

This officer drafted a telegram for the Secretary's signature, directing the Legation to pursue a vigorous investigation into the facts and suggesting specific lines of investigation. The telegram was submitted to the Assistant Chief and Chief of the Near Eastern Division for initialing. They requested revision. Once the text had been agreed upon in the Near Eastern Division, the Chief of the Division signed the Secretary's name to the telegram, adding his own initials in parentheses to show that he accepted responsibility. The telegram was thereafter discussed with the Legal Division (now the Legal Adviser's Office) officer specializing in Near Eastern Affairs, and with the desk officer for Italy in the European Division. (As seen on the chart, the Italian desk would now be under the new Southern European Division.) The last-mentioned officer decided whether the telegram should be submitted for approval to the Assistant Chief or Chief of the European Division. The telegram was finally submitted to one of the most Argus-eyed officers of the Department, the Chief of the Division of Co-ordination and Review, for scrutiny to determine whether full co-ordination had been effected and whether the text conformed with the Department's accepted style, language, and general form. From there the telegram was sent to the code room to be encoded and despatched by telegraph.

The full and complete report of the incident forwarded to the Department by the Legation in Cairo revealed that a strong protest to the Italian Government, including a claim for compensation for the damage done to the American missionary property, was warranted. The note of protest, framed in careful diplomatic language, was drafted by the desk officer on Egypt, submitted to the Assistant Chief and Chief of the Near Eastern Division, the Legal Adviser, the desk officer on Italy, and to the Assistant Chief and Chief of the European Division. It was made the subject of personal discussion by the Chief of the Near Eastern Division with the Under Secretary. When final approval was obtained, the note was incorporated in a telegram to the Embassy in Rome with instructions for its presentation to the Italian Foreign Office.

This minor episode illustrates the handling of a problem on the lower level of policy. It may be thought that the necessity of having so simple a question of policy pass in review through so many hands is excessively cautious. The answer is that the Government's business, unlike private business, demands the most careful review, particularly in the field of foreign affairs. The most seemingly unimportant matter may have unexpected implications which come to light only after searching scrutiny by all those officers whose knowledge may have a bearing upon it. Let us now consider the method of dealing with a question of policy on the highest level.

The British White Paper on Palestine of 1939, restricted immigration, and evoked an unparalleled volume of protests to the Department. More than 100,000 communications were received on the subject, including several hundred letters from Congressmen, governors of states, and other public officials. It was obviously impossible to reply to each letter individually, as had been previously the uniform practice of the Department. The volume of correspondence occasioned the formulation of a new policy in this respect. Officers no longer are required to reply individually to communications which involve mass issues except in the case of correspondence from public officials, or from private individuals when it is clear that they have written to give expression to their private views, without organized instruction.

The volume of protests clearly necessitated a review of the United States Government's policy on Palestine. At a conference participated in by the desk officer on Palestine, the Acting Chief of the Division of Near Eastern Affairs and a member of the Legal Division, it was decided that a public statement of policy was desirable. This was carefully drafted in the Division of Near Eastern Affairs and, as the issue directly affected the United Kingdom, the text was submitted to the Chief of the Division of European Affairs (United Kingdom matters would now concern the new Division of British Commonwealth Affairs) as well as to the Legal Division. Embodying as the text did a statement of high policy, it was discussed and cleared at a conference of the highest officials of the Department, including certain Division Chiefs, the Legal Adviser, an Assistant Secretary, the Under Secretary, and the Secretary himself. Finally, so important was the proposed statement of policy, the Secretary, Mr. Hull, deemed it necessary to clear it with the President.

The foregoing incidents are typical illustrations of the working operations of the Department before the creation of the geographical Offices, and show how it deals with the hundreds of problems affecting our foreign relations upon which it is called daily to act.

Naturally, hundreds of decisions of a routine character, which do not involve a departure from clearly defined and accepted policy, are taken daily by the various desk officers. These men are for the most part Foreign Service officers dealing with particular countries. They handle the in-and-out flow of correspondence relating to American foreign relations with those countries. Such officers must have an intimate acquaintance with the particular countries or areas for which they are responsible, which can only be adequately gained by service in the field. They must be prepared to answer offhand and at a moment's notice, political, economic, and other questions that may be raised regarding the countries with which they are concerned.

An officer in the Legal Adviser's Office may telephone the officer concerned with French North Africa and ask for information concerning the difference in political status of Morocco, Algeria, and Tunisia with reference to France. The desk officer is expected to be able to tell his legal colleague that, while Algeria is assimilated administratively to France, the relation of Tunisia to France is that of a protectorate, as is also that of Morocco—the United States enjoying a greater measure of treaty rights in Morocco than in either Tunisia or Algeria.

On the eve of the war a prominent publicist telephoned the desk officer for Egypt and asked many searching questions regarding the organization and administration of the Suez Canal. When the publicist commented with some surprise upon the fullness and exactness of the information given him, the officer explained that he had served five years in Egypt and that, as the desk officer for Egypt, he had to be thoroughly informed on the status of an international waterway so vitally affecting the destiny of the country through which it passed.

On economic matters, the Under Secretary for Economic Affairs is consulted, since he is responsible for economic policy. Decisions in other areas, such as public affairs, are referred to the appropriate Assistant Secretary. No departmental officer, short of an Assistant Secretary, can determine American policy, and no Foreign Service officer in the field, even though serving as ambassador or minister, would consider departing from the Department's instructions or have the power to influence or change its policy except under extraordinary circumstances.

When the burden of decisions placed upon the higher officials of the Department is crushing and the number of Assistant Secretaries is insufficient, decisions affecting policy are sometimes made by Directors of Offices, and even lower down in the hierarchical scale, in sheer desperation to get things done. The result is that instead of policy being made first, decisions affecting policy have precedence; instead of policy governing decisions, decisions begin to govern policy; instead of policy being determined by executives, with officers at lower levels making decisions conformable with existing policy, the former find themselves making policies and decisions in some matters, while in others subordinates make decisions which determine policy. When such a situation prevails, decisions are made in good faith and not in any conspiratorial spirit to serve the particular aims of prejudice or party. Moreover, decisions made on lower levels are always subject to review and revision by policy-making officers.

There is a widespread and popular misconception that Foreign Service officers in the field have wide latitude in the determination and execution of policy. This erroneous belief results in misplaced blame: For example, the identification in the public mind of American policy toward the Franco regime, with the American Ambassador in Madrid and his staff, and our French North African policy in 1941-1943 with those officers in the field charged with its execution. It cannot be too strongly emphasized that American policy in these and other foreign relations is determined by the President, and that the Department and its officers in the field are only the executants of that policy.

It is true that officers in the field, and those officers in the Department dealing with such questions, from the lowest to the highest level, often have some part in *shaping* American policy by the reports and recommendations they may make. Thus, in 1941 and 1942, American policy in regard to the question of leadership in French North Africa, was undoubtedly influenced by the reports received from Foreign Service officers in that area. The reports were reflections of facts. The Vichy government had deliberately staffed the French Army and administration in North Africa with its loyal supporters; de Gaullists, with few exceptions, had been consigned to prison. Our Foreign Service officers had far more sympathy for de Gaulle than for the officers who had served Vichy. It would have been, however, a complete distortion of existing facts and circumstances had they represented the French officers who were in command in French North Africa in 1941 and 1942, as more ready to rally to General de Gaulle than to General Giraud.

The Assistant Secretary of State for the administration of the Department is responsible for implementing and directing the execution of policies established by the President, or by the Secretary and Under Secretaries of State, or the Assistant Secretaries who specialize in economic affairs, public affairs, and other policy areas. The Board of the Foreign Service acts as a connecting link with the top policy officers of the

Department. It is a non-Foreign Service Board, and brings an objective point of view to the administration of the Service. It insures responsiveness in the Service to the policies of the Secretary and his top staff officers. Its members are three Assistant Secretaries (including the Assistant Secretary for administration), the Director General of the Foreign Service, and representatives of the Department of Commerce, Department of Agriculture, Department of Labor, and, by invitation, other agencies particularly interested in matters brought up before the Board. The Board makes recommendations to the Secretary concerning policies affecting the personnel administration of the Service.

The practical administration of the Foreign Service is in the hands of its Director General. He co-ordinates the activities of the Service with the needs of the Department and of other Government agencies, and directs the performance by officers and employees of the Service of the duties imposed on them by law, order, or regulation, or by any international agreement to which the United States is a party. The Secretary of State has wide discretion and great authority in prescribing regulations for the Foreign Service. Most of the information on which these regulations are based, and most of the preliminary development of the regulations themselves are the work of the Director General and his subordinates in the Department.

The Director General is the ranking position in the Foreign Service corresponding to a chief-of-staff. He is, therefore, always a Foreign Service officer, appointed from the Class of career minister or Class 1.

His second in command is the Deputy Director general, who need not be a career officer. He may hold his position more than four years and thus provide continuity of administration.

Under the Director and his Deputy works the large headquarters, or home office staff of the Service. The members of this staff are the central cells of a nerve center whose neurons radiate to every corner of the globe; if a third secretary gets put in jail in Sofia, or a vice-consul's wife has a baby in Bogotá, it becomes their problem. If the Secretary of the Treasury requires a confidential report on a trading firm in the Malay Archipelago, that is their problem, too. They disburse millions of dollars every year, and regulate the work of thousands they never see.

The duties of the Director General's office are so varied and complex that a detailed account of them would seem but a sterile dissection of the anatomy of bureaucracy. The daily activities of the home office take on life and meaning only for those who have worked in or with the Department of State. The general functions of the home office, on the other hand, are both interesting and illuminating.

One of the most important of these functions derives from the Director General's duty to "co-ordinate the activities of the Service with the needs of the Department and other Government agencies." It is not enough that policy makers and administrators work together at the apex of the hierarchical pyramid; subordinates at all levels must also be in step. To take an example from the bottom; the work of clerks and stenographers in the various offices and divisions must be co-ordinated through a system of routing, filing, and code symbols or the paper work will descend into chaos.

Higher in the scale of work, but actually no more essential, come co-ordination in policy matters and reporting. Regular contact must be maintained with all responsible divisions of the Department to see to it that changes in procedure and policy are promptly put into instructions for Foreign Service officers abroad. The "geographic and functional" divisions of the Department (and other Government agencies as well), are responsible for guiding Foreign Service reporting in subject-matter fields, and for drafting instructions and evaluating the reports. The consumer, in other words, says what he wants and how he wants it. The home office of the Foreign Service must not only keep in close touch with these other divisions and agencies; it must also screen the requests for reports to prevent duplication and other nonessential work, co-ordinate the requests into a workable set of instructions, and dispatch them to the proper missions overseas.

The Foreign Service officers abroad must be kept informed as to how their work is being used in the Department, and how effective it is. When an officer comes home, he must be brought together for consultation with the people in Government who depend upon him for information.

Another of the home office's main functions is planning. The Service can only be effective if it is continually adapted to world conditions, which have never been more restless. To adapt, it is necessary to foresee. The Service, therefore, must study itself continually in the light of predictable events; plan changes long in advance and take the preliminary steps which will result in the right moves at the right time.

The current deployment and management of Service personnel is another large problem. It is not enough, for example, to know that a Spanish-speaking officer of Class 3, with some knowledge of economics and a flair for getting along with influential politicians, is needed in Mexico City. The officer's development is to be considered. It might, in the long-term interests of the Service, be advisable to send the best available man to Madrid, and to send another qualified man to Mexico City.

The elaborate and critical machinery of recruitment and promotion must be maintained in smooth working order. And the Foreign Service Institute presents administrative problems which would be faced by the head of any first-class university, along with some peculiar ones of its own.

The housekeeping duties of the home office—the housing, feeding, paying, and general care of thousands of employees thinly scattered all over the globe—are more intricate than those of most big businesses and Government agencies. If a tidal wave in Santo Domingo swamps the home of a Foreign Service officer, the home office must see to it that he is reimbursed for the loss of his personal property. If adequate food is not to be had in the shops and restaurants of Athens, a commissary must be maintained.

There was a time—and not very long ago, either, since the purchase of buildings for our missions was not authorized until 1926—when Foreign Service officers had to use their wits to keep a decent roof over their heads. Consider, for example, the case of the Minister to Morocco and the enterprising brothel-keepers of Tangier.

At that time the United States possessed in Tangier only the property which had been presented by the Sultan of Morocco in 1820. It was in the native quarter, on a street so narrow that only pedestrians could pass one another. Word came to the minister that the building opposite was to be turned into a house of ill-fame.

There was in Tangier a wealthy Jewish merchant who had long sought American protection. The minister went to him and proposed that the merchant be made an American protégé, under the right then as now enjoyed by the United States to appoint twelve subjects of the Sultan to this peculiar status. In return, the merchant was to purchase the prospective bawdyhouse. The merchant was overjoyed, and the building today houses the main part of the chancery.

The United States now houses its representatives more securely. Since 1926 some $25,000,000 have been spent for buildings used by Foreign Service officers, and it is planned to spend $45,000,000 more by 1956. These plans and the real estate management necessary for acquisition and upkeep of the buildings are also the work of the home office of the Foreign Service.

IV

THE FOREIGN SERVICE AND
OTHER GOVERNMENT AGENCIES

THE FOREIGN SERVICE has been called the eyes and the ears of the United States Government abroad. It supplies information to all Government agencies and to the Congress. This information has three general uses (1) enlightenment of the interested sections of the American public; for example, agricultural information for farmers, and trade information for businessmen; (2) the shaping of domestic policy in response to world conditions and the activities of particular nations; for example, the balance in farm production toward which the Department of Agriculture strives, changes with the world crop situation and with protective measures taken by particular countries; (3) the shaping of foreign policies and policy instruments which must be co-ordinated with domestic policies and laws, and thus involve collaboration between the State Department and other Government agencies; for example, the "Good Neighbor" policy, and Reciprocal Trade Treaties. These three functions—public enlightenment, the formation of domestic policy, and the co-ordination of foreign

[49]

and domestic policy, make the reports of Foreign Service officers an important factor in almost every phase of the nation's public life.

In addition, the Foreign Service executes abroad certain laws and regulations which at home are the province of other agencies; for example, laws and regulations concerning sailors and shipping, immigration, etc. These services demand very close working relationships between the State Department and other agencies.

During the past quarter century the increasing interdependence of the world and the growing power of the United States have made the work done by the Foreign Service for other Government agencies increasingly complex and important. Other agencies, therefore, have a vital interest in the development of the Service, in the way its members do their work, and in the selection and training of officers. This interest is recognized both in law and in actual administration.

The Foreign Service Act of 1946 (Sec. 311) states that:

The officers and employees of the Service shall, under such regulations as the President may prescribe, perform duties and functions in behalf of any Government agency or any other establishment of the Government requiring their services, including those in the legislative and judicial branches, but the absence of such regulations shall not preclude officers and employees of the Service from acting for and on behalf of any such Government agency or establishment whenever it shall, through the Department, request their services.

The Act of 1946 also legally established the Board of the Foreign Service (described in Chapter III). This group makes administrative policy in the light of the Government's total needs; its membership includes representatives of several government agencies. The Board of Examiners for the Foreign Service, which provides for and supervises the conduct of such examinations as are given for admission to the Service, which controls recruitment policy and standards, may also include representatives of other agencies. Various interdepartmental committees are established from time to time as circumstances make it necessary for agencies to get together with the Foreign Service on particular areas of policy, on the special training of Foreign Service officers, and other matters.

Lower down among the stratified levels of responsibility are liaison officers; representatives of the Foreign Service working with and sometimes physically in, other agencies; and representatives of other agencies being attached to the Foreign Service. The home office of the Foreign Service customarily maintains a "liaison headquarters" where these representatives do their work.

Co-operation is also furthered by the Reserve officers of the Foreign Service. A great many of these officers are drawn from other Government agencies, to which they return when their tours of duty in the Foreign Service are ended. Foreign Service officers also serve for periods ranging up to four years with other agencies.

Almost any report from officers abroad may contain material useful to some other Government agency beside the State Department. The thousands of telegrams and despatches received daily from the Foreign Service posts abroad are therefore examined as they come in to determine their various destinations. For example, a despatch from Montevideo on the economic policies of the Uruguayan Government may be useful to the Departments of Commerce, Agriculture, Treasury, Labor, and the Tariff Commission, and to the War and Navy Departments. The despatch is received in hectograph and the necessary number of copies quickly run off and distributed. This is standard procedure governing all reports from the field. Political reports are the only ones generally reserved for the exclusive use of the Department of State, but when any of these has a bearing upon the military situation, a copy may go to the War Department; when a political report has a bearing upon the financial state of the country concerned, a copy may go to the Treasury Department. In addition to this constant and routine flow of material through the Department of State to every agency of the Government having any interest in foreign developments, the Foreign Service renders regular reports needed by other agencies, and special reports on request.

The Department of Agriculture, through the Office of Foreign Agricultural Relations, is responsible for analyzing and disseminating to the public, foreign information concerning agriculture. This information is gathered abroad and reported by Foreign Service officers who specialize in agricultural problems.

The traditional field in which agricultural attachés abroad formerly specialized, was "foreign competition and demand," covering all foreign developments affecting the export movement of United States agricultural products, and the movement into United States markets of agricultural products competing with domestic production.

In the period 1920-1930 agricultural attachés were considered to be adequately discharging their functions if they observed promptly and reported accurately such relatively simple developments as variations in crop output and livestock numbers, changes in purchasing power and related factors resulting from the unrestricted interplay of natural and economic forces. The significance of these factors declined after 1930 as world economy sank further into depression, and economic nationalism raised higher and more formidable barriers against international trade. Agricultural importing countries increased the tariff protection of their farmers, while exporting countries adopted countermeasures to improve the competitive position of their own products in international markets.

The reports submitted by American missions abroad had an important influence on agricultural policy in the United States. As export markets shrank, measures were adopted by the Government to divert crop lands into soil conservation work, to support farm prices by loans, and to increase domestic consumption through the food stamp and other plans.

The reciprocal trade agreement program was undertaken to remove some of the economic road blocks which had been thrown up by nations to protest their misery. Officials of the Departments of State, Agriculture, Commerce, and the Tariff Commission, met in committee with Foreign Service officers for the drafting of these agreements.

The outbreak of war and the entrance of the United States created a host of new and intricate problems. Not least was the need of greatly expanding the Foreign Service to undertake the many new tasks devolving upon it. This was accomplished by the creation of an Auxiliary Foreign Service.

The merging of American national economy with the United Nations' supply system meant a re-examination of food supplies, arranging for their acquisition and transport and keeping Washington informed generally about developments vital to the prosecution of the war.

The wartime interruption of international trade and the part played by the Foreign Service in developing new sources of supply of curtailed agricultural products may be illustrated, to cite one example, by the work done in the case of vegetable oils. Foreign Service officers worked closely with wartime missions in encouraging a larger output of such oils in friendly territories, particularly in the American Republics.

In addition to agricultural appraisals of foreign countries, industrial appraisals by Foreign Service officers have, in many cases, great significance for American agriculture. For instance, information which officers supply on the state of the textile industry in the country of their assignment, makes it possible to estimate the amount of cotton which may be needed during the next year and what proportion of the demand the United States will be called on to supply. Reporting by Foreign Service officers on agricultural policy is of greater significance to American farmers than reporting of any other factor. Continuation of the self-sufficiency programs of importing countries means continued restrictions on imports of most agricultural commodities from the United States after immediate postwar shortages have been met. Continuation of aids to the overseas movement of surplus supplies presages close competition for a place in sharply restricted markets. Accordingly, prompt and accurate reporting on these subjects constitutes a substantial contribution to the agricultural policies adopted by the United States which must ultimately affect the lives of the whole population.

With a domestic output more than sufficient to meet a high level of domestic consumption, can we anticipate opportunities to sell abroad on acceptable terms or are we to be faced with the decision that our volume of production is, in fact, burdensome economically and must be restricted by reason of the impossibility of persuading other governments to ease their restrictive international practices? Decisions such as these cannot be made without the information which Foreign Service officers are constantly furnishing the policy-making officials of the Government through the Department of State.

One of the greatest incentives to the removal of measures founded upon economic nationalism would be the establishment of such an effective international security system that economic self-sufficiency would no longer be deemed essential

[54]

to the defense of the state. Artificial barriers to world trade would be let down, once the fear of war was removed—thus ushering in an unparalleled period of world prosperity from which all would benefit. Both the particular work of the agricultural attaché and the more general efforts of the Foreign Service in developing greater international confidence and understanding, vitally affect the American farmer. It is in appreciation of this fact that measures are constantly being taken to strengthen co-operation between the Foreign Service and the Agriculture Department.

Probably no other agency of the Government is so closely linked with the Foreign Service as is the Department of Commerce.

By United States Statute the Department of Commerce, established in 1903, is specifically charged with the duty of fostering and developing foreign and domestic trade, mining, manufacturing, shipping industries, and transportation facilities of the United States. Until 1912 these activities were mainly confined to the Bureau of Manufactures which, in that year, was merged with the Bureau of Statistics into a single Bureau of Foreign and Domestic Commerce (now the Office of International Trade). This Bureau is the connecting link between the Department of Commerce and the Foreign Service on the commerce side; the link on the Foreign Service side is the economic reporting and trade promotion system, manned by specially trained officers both abroad and in the home office.

The Department of Commerce has been made by Congress the sole means for the public dissemination of the economic and commercial reports of Foreign Service officers. Such reports are published in the *Foreign Commerce Weekly,* and as separate documents when especially important. The Department of Commerce also uses material furnished by Foreign Service

[55]

officers in replying to letters of inquiry from American firms or individuals.

While the Foreign Service of the United States acts as the eyes and ears of the American business community abroad, the personnel of the Office of International Trade and the regional offices of the Department of Commerce, located in the principal commercial centers of the United States, act as the eyes and ears of the Foreign Service at home. For Department of Commerce representatives gather the information requested of the Foreign Service by foreign businessmen. This service is of great value, as the aggregate number of requests received for information from foreign businessmen regarding American sources of supply, technical developments, and potential representatives is at least equal to the number of inquiries received from American businessmen for similar information from abroad.

The Secretary of Commerce makes direct requests of the Foreign Service for information regarding commercial and economic developments abroad. All outstanding circular instructions and the Foreign Service Regulations pertaining to commercial and economic reporting have been drafted either by, or in consultation with, the appropriate commodity and foreign trade specialists of the Department of Commerce, which in effect still continues to exercise, as it was meant to do (under the reorganization plan of 1939), more or less control over the activities of the commercial and economic offices of the Foreign Service of the United States.

The reports called for in the standing instructions to the field provide for the prompt reporting of commercial policy and tariff and exchange developments affecting American trade; opportunities for the sale of American products; and the availability of certain commodities for sale in the United States; detailed data in the housing field; and factual surveys covering the demand for American construction materials and technical skills and services. Officers working in the commercial and economic services of the Foreign Service are likewise called upon to report regularly on foreign economic conditions; to help businessmen judge for themselves the potential opportunities afforded by foreign markets; submit detailed analyses of foreign financial trends and developments; and to observe in detail conditions and developments in foreign industries. All of this material from the Foreign Service is promptly made available to American business interests through Department of Commerce publications, and direct contact with American foreign traders and businessmen. When specific information is required by American business interests, a simple request made at any of the regional offices of the Department of Commerce or direct to the office at Washington will immediately bring into play the resources of the Foreign Service to answer the inquiry. Many of the requests made by American firms for information regarding foreign firms or conditions abroad, can readily be answered from the mass of detailed and up-to-date material on file in the office at Washington. In the interests of time and economy both the Departments of State and Commerce urge American business interests to submit their requests either to the regional offices or to the office in Washington before corresponding with our missions abroad.

Another valuable service provided to American business as a result of the co-operation between the Departments of State and Commerce, is the tours made by commercial and economic experts of the Foreign Service to the leading commercial centers of the United States. They meet with businessmen and give them first-hand impressions and factual reports on foreign firms and developments.

Except for the armed services, the Treasury Department is

the only Government agency which maintains independent attachés abroad. These representatives are stationed at a few key posts, such as London and Paris. However, the Foreign Service furnishes the Treasury Department with most of the services performed abroad on its behalf. So extensive indeed is the contribution made by the Foreign Service that there seems no reason any longer to maintain independent Treasury attachés. These might be either absorbed into the Foreign Service, as were the Commerce and Agriculture attachés in 1939, or they might be assigned from the Department of State.

Besides reporting upon financial, monetary, customs, tariff, fiscal and general economic developments in their respective districts, Foreign Service officers are required to perform a wide variety of functions on behalf of the Treasury. These include the administration of American income-tax laws, the certification of invoices covering imports into the United States, investigation of the costs of production, market values, tariff discrimination, exchange control regulations, currency depreciation and dumping, detection and reporting of plans and channels of smuggling, the detection and reporting of counterfeiting of United States money and securities.

Foreign Service officers constantly help the Treasury Department in its fight to control narcotics. Their prompt reports often lead to the seizure of important shipments of smuggled narcotics; large narcotic rings in the United States are frequently broken up in consequence of evidence uncovered by Foreign Service officers abroad. So close is the co-operation in this field, that when the Treasury Department was seeking a Commissioner of Narcotics some years ago its choice fell upon Mr. Harry J. Anslinger, a Foreign Service officer, who was at first loaned to the Treasury and who afterwards resigned and became a Treasury official.

Mr. Anslinger was the first Foreign Service officer to be

loaned to another agency of the Government. The precedent thus established has been followed subsequently to a greater and greater extent.

For example, Mr. H. Merle Cochran, during the late 1930's when he was First Secretary of the Embassy in Paris, devoted practically all of his time to work on behalf of the Treasury. Among other important services he acted for the Treasury in negotiating the Tripartite Monetary Agreement between France, the United Kingdom, and the United States. He advised Secretary Morgenthau by transatlantic telephone concerning the current European situation during that period. He was loaned to the Treasury in 1939, became a Technical Assistant to Mr. Morgenthau, and in the autumn of 1941 went to China. He brought back from Generalissimo Chiang Kai-Shek a schedule of financial assistance needed in the war against Japan, and helped to make the arrangements by which this aid was rendered.

At the request of the Treasury, three Foreign Service officers were especially assigned to London, Paris, and Berlin to specialize in work for the Treasury in financial and monetary matters.

A notable instance of the use of the Foreign Service in implementing certain extraordinary tasks undertaken by the Treasury Department is to be had in the part played by Foreign Service officers during the war in the administration abroad of the control of foreign funds.

In 1940 the United States began to block the funds of certain countries to prevent their use in a way detrimental to American interests. This was a Treasury operation, but the principal task of applying these measures of control outside United States territory fell upon Foreign Service officers. The missions abroad had a determining voice in decisions to include individuals and firms in the "black list"; the missions could and frequently did take the initiative in proposing names for the list. Once on the black list the individual or company could not draw upon any American funds, except under a license issued by a Foreign Service officer.

Probably no service rendered by the Foreign Service more directly affects the welfare of the people of the United States than the health reports rendered to the Public Health Service of the Federal Security Agency. Sanitary reports, including statistics on communicable diseases, are submitted periodically by every Foreign Service post in the world; unusual epidemics are reported by telegraph. The germs of yellow fever, cholera, plague, or any other epidemic disease may easily be invisible freight on transocean planes, and it is literally vital to be warned that they may be headed our way.

Co-operation between the Foreign Service and the War and Navy Departments in the field is of two kinds. Foreign Service officers work with the military and naval attachés assigned to diplomatic missions. Pertinent reports by Foreign Service officers flow into Washington and are channeled to the War and Navy Departments.

To most American diplomatic missions are assigned one or more military and naval attachés, the number depending upon the importance of the country and its military and naval establishments. Although such attachés receive their instructions from and report directly to their respective departments, they exercise their duties under the general supervision of the chief of mission. In the matter of precedence they rank next in succession after Foreign Service officers of the rank of counselor, or, where there is no counselor, after the senior secretary of the mission, irrespective of the military rank that they may hold.*

* See Appendix C for comparative rank of Foreign Service and Army officers, and military honors paid the former.

During the Second World War there was, in some active theaters, a certain amount of friction due to fundamentally different viewpoints, and very different operating methods. In war the Army must reach limited objectives quickly; the Foreign Service must at all times consider the long-term relations between our country and others. The Army operates by direct action; the Foreign Service by negotiation. However, at diplomatic missions where military and naval attachés were assigned during the war there was the closest possible co-operation, and a constant exchange of information. To avoid duplication of work and at the same time escape any possibility of information of value being overlooked in such exchange in Washington, attachés invited their departments' attention to pertinent telegrams or despatches emanating from the chiefs of mission. Similarly, attachés brought to the attention of the chiefs of mission any information collected by them bearing, however remotely, upon the political or economic situation of the country to which the mission was accredited.

The co-operation of the Foreign Service with the War and Navy Departments and their representatives went far beyond reporting. The Foreign Service was active in preparing the way for our troops and in smoothing their way after they landed.

Prior to the United States' entry into the war, many Foreign Service establishments, particularly the consulates general and consulates where no military or naval attachés were assigned, were the sole sources in their areas of military and strategic information of importance to the American Government. Foreign Service officers were everywhere notably active in the implementation of the American policy of according all aid short of war to the nations resisting aggression by the Axis.

The information furnished by State Department representatives in French North Africa and West Africa and in Tangier from 1940 to the time of the landings in November, 1942, together with information forwarded by the American Embassy in Vichy until its closing at the end of 1941, has been described by the War and Navy Departments as of incalculable value. In Greenland, Foreign Service officers were in daily contact with representatives of the War and Navy Departments, working toward the settlement with the local authorities of problems arising out of the occupation. In Iceland, the American mission performed similar service. And at Paramaribo in Surinam (Dutch Guiana), the American Vice-Consul in charge, Carl Norden, rendered exceptional services in preparing the way for the friendly reception of American forces. After their arrival, Mr. Norden's work consisted almost exclusively in the conduct of negotiations between the Government of Surinam and the Commanding Officer of the American Forces.

In Tangier the Legation succeeded in obtaining from the Spanish Moroccan authorities an undertaking not to fire upon planes and blimps of the American submarine patrol.

With the landing of American forces in active war theaters, Foreign Service officers were detailed to act as political advisers to the American Commanding Officers. Mr. Robert Murphy became Political Adviser to General Eisenhower on the occasion of the North African landings, and Mr. Maynard Barnes served in the same capacity with Admiral Glassford in French West Africa. With the war's end, Mr. Murphy became Political Adviser to the Commanding General of the American Forces in occupied Germany; Mr. John G. Erhardt was named in a similar capacity with General Mark Clark in Austria, and Mr. George Atcheson ·with General Douglas MacArthur in Japan.

It is the official view of the State Department that co-operation between the three services should be even more intimate than in the past. Each year a group of Foreign Service officers are assigned to the National War College, and selected Army and Navy officers may be assigned to the Foreign Service Institute. Thus, through greater mutual understanding, greater effectiveness will be fostered.

V

THE PROFESSION AND PRACTICE
OF DIPLOMACY

THE ART of diplomacy consists of making the policy of one government understood and if possible accepted by other governments. Policy is thus the substance of foreign relations; diplomacy proper is the process by which policy is carried out.

American foreign policy has its source in laws passed by Congress and—most especially—in the President's beliefs concerning what should be done to achieve the prosperity and well-being of the American people. The President is aided in forming policy by the Secretary of State and other high officials of the Department. But although diplomats execute rather than frame policy, they nevertheless play an important part in shaping it. For their reports from overseas are raw materials from which policies are made, and to execute any policy, it must be adjusted with others and reinterpreted in the light of conditions at the point of application.

All American Foreign Service officers are diplomats; all of them perform the four basic phases of diplomacy—representa-

[64]

tion, negotiation, reporting, and protection of American interests abroad. However, the work of ambassadors and ministers is not only more important; it is more evenly divided among the four phases. A vice-consul has relatively little representation to perform—unless he is in charge of a post. He may have little to do in the way of negotiation. His duties may lie almost exclusively in protecting American interests. An ambassador or minister will be occupied constantly with all four functions.

The functions of representation, negotiation, and reporting are so intertwined that, in actual practice, they are difficult to separate. A Foreign Service officer's success in any of these phases depends very largely on his ability to know the people of the country where he is assigned and to make the most of a wide range of contacts.

These contacts begin with representation. In a capital, the ambassador or one of his aides is called upon to represent the United States at all ceremonial functions in which the foreign diplomatic corps participates. At the smaller posts, the ranking consular officer plays the ceremonial role. The manner in which Foreign Service officers play their parts at these functions is extremely important. Their duty is to establish and further good will toward the United States, without which no mission can function successfully. And since—in a sense—they *are* the United States in the countries of their assignment, they must comport themselves accordingly, not only in ceremonial contacts, but in all their social relationships.

Through representation, the diplomat makes his first connections with his colleagues in other missions and with the government officials of the country of his assignment. But his connections with them cannot stop there. Nor can he limit his contacts to the persons whom ceremony puts in his way. To perform the functions of representation is to be introduced to a country—not to know it.

[65]

Until the time of the French Revolution, the contacts of ambassadors and their suites were limited almost exclusively to court circles: the sovereign, his principal ministers and those persons enjoying influence with the sovereign by reason of their official or social position. It was these alone who made policy and so long as an ambassador and his staff remained in contact with the court, the duties of his mission could be adequately discharged.

The tradition thus established died hard. Even after courts had begun to lose their influence in the nineteenth century, the tendency of most diplomatic officers was to limit their intercourse in the capitals to a narrow, exclusive circle of the so-called "best society" long after this "best society" had ceased to exercise a controlling influence on the shape of affairs. So it was that until only a few years ago, the diplomatic corps in most capitals was accustomed to confine its social activities to diplomatic colleagues, the senior officials of the country, and to affluent private individuals disposed to entertain on a lavish scale.

Notwithstanding the absence of a court society in the United States (or, perhaps, because of it), American diplomats were all too often caught up and enmeshed in a round of banal social life at a foreign capital. The organization of the American Foreign Service prior to 1924, with a maximum salary scale of $3,000, closed the door to all except the sons of America's wealthiest families. An officer named to Paris or London could not meet his barest living expenses out of his salary. As late as 1946, the post of counselor of embassy in those capitals involved such a heavy financial outlay for the entertainment necessary to discharge the essential functions of representation, that these posts were often refused by able men who found it impossible to sustain the burden.

The trend toward government by the people has vastly increased the responsibilities of a chief of mission and made his ability to establish fruitful contacts with all sections of the population vitally important to his government. As Ambassador Jusserand has noted: "Experience has already shown and will more and more show that no invention, no telephone, no aeroplane, no wireless, will ever replace the knowledge of a country and the understanding of a people's dispositions. The importance of persuading a prince and his ministers has diminished; that of understanding a nation has increased. The temper, qualities, and limitations of many a man can be divined on short acquaintance; those of a nation need a longer contact." *

If one reads the volume of *Foreign Relations of the U. S. 1916-1918* on Russia, it will be strikingly apparent that few if any of our officers serving at that time in Russia had contact with any but the upper stratum of the population. This explains, in part, why the United States Government was so grievously misinformed of the significance of the Russian Revolution. This ignorance of the Russian nation as a whole was not, of course, peculiar to the officers serving in Russia, nor to the American diplomatic service. Most of the foreign services of the time were equally narrow.

Before the appointment of Mr. William S. Culbertson as American Minister to Rumania in 1926, the American Legation was frequented by the *boyars* of Rumanian society, and had little contact with the world outside of the court and Rumanian official society. Mr. Culbertson introduced a breath of fresh air in the Legation by throwing it open to teachers, doctors, writers, and members of all political parties. He thus attained a position of influence as a diplomat such as few if any foreign officers had ever before enjoyed in that country.

* Jusserand, "School for Ambassadors," page 67.

By maintaining the social contacts necessary for representation an able officer gains important sources of information which assist him in his negotiations and reporting functions. Some of the most important information which Foreign Service officers obtain is through the social contacts formed and extended at social gatherings.

George Wadsworth, one of this country's outstanding career officers, said, when asked by a junior member of his staff, whether certain persons might be useful contacts: "I have yet to meet anyone in this country not worthy of cultivation in furthering a study of Egypt and its complex social background." It was Mr. Wadsworth who advised one of his subordinates to accept every social invitation which he might receive as a means of extending his knowledge of the life of Egypt and its people.

At large receptions and dinners where tired dowagers descant upon their servant problems, or their terror of the Left-wing movements in Europe and Asia, a Foreign Service officer may hear something important from a fellow sufferer. More profitable may be a small gathering of labor leaders or journalists whom the officer has brought together to draw out in discussion, or a group of the prominent younger leaders of the Arab League.

In these days it is not sufficient to limit oneself to the conventional social life of a post; the officer, who is alert and far-seeing, takes the initiative in establishing and extending the range of his social contacts. He deliberately seeks introductions to people who may further his understanding of the country in which he is stationed or who may aid him in his reporting or other functions.

Not only do social contacts afford a means for the Foreign Service officer to obtain information about the country of his assignment but they also afford opportunity to build up good will for the United States. One of the prime objectives of Foreign Service officers is that of establishing close and fruitful contacts conducive to the promotion of American interests. A prime means to this end is building up friendly sentiment toward the United States among the Foreign Service officers' acquaintances.

However, those who, on the diplomat's first arrival in the country, appear the most eager to make his acquaintance and to communicate their ideas are often least to be trusted. Their professions are often insincere and their intelligence false. They are usually the first whom the diplomat wishes to shake off whenever he has been so imprudent as to give them credit for sincerity. The efforts of collaboration-tainted American expatriates and native French to "use" the Paris Embassy when it was first reopened after World War II is striking evidence of both the diplomat's need to take care, and the value of experience. People who had been most ostentatious and loud in welcoming the Germans and proclaiming the "new order" were the most aggressively friendly to the Americans. After the liberation, high-ranking American officers were deluged with invitations. Ambassador Caffery was too experienced to swallow this bait (as did a good many officers competent in war, but unused to representing their country). He issued orders that calling cards were not to be exchanged between himself and anyone except officials, colleagues, and persons whose status had been firmly established. Collaborators were thus prevented from boasting that they had friends in high places in the Paris Embassy.

So important did negotiations loom in the early days of diplomacy, that a foreign representative was known more commonly by the term "negotiator" than by that of diplomat. The functions of the diplomat have since been extended, but negotiation has not lessened in importance.

Co-operation between nations has always been based upon agreements. The increasing complexity and the wide extension of these relations in modern times has indeed vastly increased the work of negotiation of the Foreign Service officer. Such work includes the drafting of a wide variety of bilateral and multilateral arrangements embodied in treaties, conventions, protocols, and other documents of a political, economic, and social nature. Their subject matter ranges from the creation of an international security organization, through territorial changes, establishment of rules to govern international civil aviation, shipping and telecommunications, and the adjustment of international commercial relationships, to such particular matters as immigration, double taxation, waterway rights, tourist travel, and exchange control. Almost the entire gamut of human activities is covered.

While modern communications may have tended in some degree to limit the wide independence formerly enjoyed by the diplomatic negotiator, no mechanical substitute has yet been found for the interplay of human qualities which may make or mar the successful conclusion of an international contract. Whatever guidance the telephone or cable instruction may give, the conduct of negotiations still calls for training, knowledge, precision, discernment, prudence, calm, patience, good temper, tact, and industry—the basic virtues of the diplomat. The preservation and furtherance of American interests demand a clear and farsighted understanding of American objectives, and the ability to report accurately and to appraise correctly the position and interests of the foreign country participating in the agreement. The most precisely drafted instructions of the Department of State will suffice little in advancing a negotiation if the Foreign Service officer is lacking in the personal attributes necessary to the successful diplomat.

Not instructions—but persistence and an understanding of people gained through long experience, won a sharp battle of wits which exemplifies negotiation. In the tense days of 1942, the American Chargé d'Affaires and the Petroleum Attaché of the Embassy in Madrid, Mr. Walter F. Smith, visited General Luis Orgaz, High Commissioner for Spanish Morocco, to get clarification of certain phases of the petroleum agreement they had together concluded some months previously. General Orgaz was adamant in maintaining his own interpretations which ran counter to that of the American diplomats. After almost two hours of discussion back and forth, the atmosphere grew tense. Mr. Smith, who in private life was Manager of the Socony-Vacuum Oil Company for the Iberian Peninsula, and who had done most of the talking, was about to rise, considering the interview terminated in failure. The Chargé d'Affaires checked him and asked Smith, whose Spanish was far superior, if he would translate a request that General Orgaz support an American proposal that an American consulate be established in Ceuta. With a horrified expression on his face, Smith expostulated that the time was anything but propitious. But he transmitted the request. General Orgaz listened impassively and when Smith had finished he fairly beamed. "Tell the American Chargé d'Affaires," he said, "I shall be delighted to give the request my most unqualified support." Smith was bewildered until the Chargé d'Affaires explained. Knowing General Orgaz, and considering in his mind how he could turn the unsatisfactory interview to American advantage, it had occurred to him that the General, having shown himself as obstinate as a mule in the interpretation of the oil agreement, would welcome an opportunity to prove to them that he was after all a reasonable man. The result was that the United States received permission to open a consulate, on the eve of the Allied landings in North Africa, at a port which might have proved of great strategic value, and where the British had been seeking for almost a year to obtain a like permission.

Negotiations in the full sense of the term are conducted not merely at the upper level of relations between States. Foreign Service officers in the field, even in the smallest consulates, are constantly engaged in negotiations at a lower level with local officials, to protect American business and other interests, to assist American citizens requiring aid in meeting local regulations, or to obtain arrangements desired abroad by American organizations.

Negotiation thus becomes almost from the beginning of his career an important part of the work of the Foreign Service officer. His work in the day-to-day lower level negotiations is practical training for eventual negotiations at a higher stage.

Diplomacy is probably more lacking in written rules for its pursuit than any other recognized profession. The reason for this absence of any fixed body of precepts, may be the fact that the successful conduct of foreign affairs depends so heavily upon the understanding of human personalities. It follows therefore that, as the human personality is of all things the most peculiarly difficult of analysis, one of the most essential qualifications of a good diplomat is the possession of insight and good judgment.

Some years ago I succeeded Mr. George Wadsworth, now Ambassador to Iraq, as senior Secretary in the American Legation in Cairo. My work had been previously limited to purely consular duties. In my apprehension over my inability to discharge the responsible diplomatic duties so unexpectedly thrust upon me, I inquired anxiously of Wadsworth for books on diplomacy to which I might refer for guidance.

"I know of no books on diplomacy on which you may rely,"

Wadsworth replied. "The only advice I can give you is that when you are confronted by a problem taxing your ingenuity, go first to the files and see if there are any precedents to guide you. If there are none, then use your common sense."

Though diplomacy has no fixed rules, great diplomats have handed down some excellent and illuminating precepts. Lord Malmesbury advises the newcomer in diplomacy: "Never to attempt to export English habits and manners, but to conform as far as possible to those of the country where you reside— to do this even in the most trivial things—to learn to speak their language, and never to sneer at what may strike you as singular or absurd. Nothing goes to conciliate so much, or to amalgamate you more cordially with its inhabitants, as this very same sacrifice of your national prejudices to *theirs*."

Callières has some equally pertinent remarks on the virtues of adaptability and humility. "The diplomatist," he writes, "must bear in mind once and for all that he is not authorized to demand that a whole nation should conform to his way of living, and that it is more reasonable, and in the long run greatly to his own comfort, to accommodate himself to foreign ways of living. He should beware of criticizing the form of government or the personal conduct of the prince to whom he is accredited. On the contrary he should always praise that which is praiseworthy without affectation and without flattery, and if he properly understands his own function he will quickly discover that there is no nation or state which has not many good points, excellent laws, charming customs as well as bad ones; and he will quickly discover that it is easy to single out the good points, and that there is no profit to be had in denouncing the bad ones, for the very good reason that nothing the diplomatist can say or will do will alter the domestic habits or laws of the country in which he lives. He

[73]

should take a pride in knowing the history of the country, so that he may be able to give the prince pleasure by praising the great feats of his ancestors, as well as for his own benefit to interpret current events in the light of the historical movements of the past."

Both Callières and Malmesbury, in common with most modern writers on the practice of diplomacy, decry the use of deception. Malmesbury warns that "no occasion, no provocation, no anxiety to rebut an unjust accusation, no idea however tempting for promoting the object you have in view, can *need,* much less justify a *falsehood.*" Callières writes that "the good negotiator will never base the success of his negotiations upon false promises or breaches of faith," adding that "dishonesty is in fact little more than a proof of the smallness of mind of him who resorts to it, and shows that he is too meagerly equipped to gain his purposes by just and reasonable methods."

There are two facets to the pursuit of truthfulness by the Foreign Service officer: there is the obligation to be scrupulously honest in his negotiations with the government to which he is accredited, and there is an equal obligation to maintain the same honesty of purpose in the reports which he submits to his own government. One of his greatest temptations is to give in to the universal human tendency to present his activities in the best light, and draft his reports in a manner which may gain him credit whatever the course developments may take. There is also the human temptation to draft reports of developments in a way which he considers may best please those at home instead of reporting the situation as it exists, however distasteful it may be to those in power. These are all temptations against which the conscientious officer must be constantly on his guard.

Malmesbury has some golden words of wisdom to give on

the necessity of precision, one of the most essential qualities in the practice of diplomacy: "In ministerial conferences, to exert every effort of *memory*, to carry away faithfully and correctly what you *hear* (what you say in them yourself you will not forget); and in drawing your report, to be most careful it should be faithful and correct. I dwell the more on this (seemingly a useless hint) because it is a most seducing temptation, and one to which we often give way most unconsciously, in order to give a better turn to a phrase, or to enhance our skill in negotiation; but we must remember we mislead and deceive our government by it."

A British official of my acquaintance received two separate memorandums made by the participants in an important discussion having to do with Anglo-Egyptian relations, the one a British diplomatic officer and the other a member of the Egyptian cabinet. My British friend stated that the two accounts of the conversation bore no recognizable relation to one another, the British diplomat having reported the conversation in a manner most favorable to himself while the Egyptian had represented himself as having scored all the points. The memoranda were, of course, equally valueless to the respective governments concerned.

The experienced diplomat is only too well aware that publicized success can be a two-edged sword which may turn and cut the ground from under his feet. There are two parties to a negotiation and two countries involved. One which crows too loudly over the benefits derived from a treaty may awaken suspicions in the other that the latter has been done in.

There is the foreign minister's pride to be considered and the *amour-propre* of the country. There are also the President at home and the members of his party who might be quick to resent any public suggestion that the American chief of mission has been responsible for the advantages gained for the United States in a particular negotiation. It must be remembered that the President, who has responsibility for the conduct of the foreign affairs of the United States, is politically vulnerable to public opinion. It is inevitable that much of the blame for foreign affairs that result unhappily should be put upon the backs of Foreign Service officers and the State Department and that the President received popular acclaim for America's diplomatic victories.

One of the cardinal characteristics of the diplomat is self-abnegation. George V. Allen, in an article for the *American Foreign Service Journal* has remarked that an acid test of loyalty of the Foreign Service officer, is the ability to carry out honestly orders and instructions with which he may not agree.

During the First World War, when Walter Hines Page was Ambassador in London, he was called upon by his government to deliver to the British Government communications on neutral rights which were in conflict with his own ideas. Page left no doubt in the mind of the British Government, when making the communications, that he was critical of them. However one may sympathize with Mr. Page, he was not discharging his duties to his government loyally. He was displaying, in this respect, one of the faults to which many noncareer officers are subject, being less schooled as they are than the professional officer in the necessity of complying with the spirit no less than the letter of instructions from their government.

The practice of diplomacy involves so wide a range of human activities and calls for the exercise of many outstanding qualities of mind and spirit that the portrait of the ideal diplomat cannot be painted—but only sketched.

Harold Nicolson has come as close as any to summing up the characteristics a great diplomatist cannot be without:

"Truth, accuracy, calm, patience, good temper, modesty, and loyalty." Anticipating the objection that he had forgotten "intelligence, knowledge, discernment, prudence, hospitality, charm, industry, courage, and even tact," Nicolson remarked that he had not forgotten them but had taken them for granted.

VI

THE PARIS EMBASSY—"SHOWCASE
OF THE DIPLOMATIC SERVICE"

T HE THREE HUNDRED and three American embassies, legations, and consulates scattered at this writing among sixty-eight countries differ not only in size, appearance, comfort, and importance; each has its own individual organization and operating method. Every mission has its own peculiar problems rising from local or national conditions and given shape by the officials with whom Foreign Service personnel must work. The personalities and capabilities of officers of the Foreign Service—particularly the chiefs of mission—play an equally important part in giving each establishment its individual character.

Of all the establishments manned by Foreign Service officers, the Embassy at Paris best illustrates how, month in and month out, the American people are served by their representatives abroad. It is one of the oldest embassies, and has carried on some of the most important negotiations in which the United States has been involved. Silas Deane, sent to Paris as commercial and political agent by the Continental Congress, was the first foreign officer of the United States to be received by a European minister. It was to Paris that Benjamin Franklin, the first American Minister, was dispatched. Thomas Jefferson and James Monroe served there.

During the years between, the Embassy's work has changed almost as much as civilization itself. No period can be typical, any more than any embassy is typical. Yet to describe the work realistically, it is necessary to fix on a moment of historic time. What is going on in Paris today is probably as interesting and as important as any of the work done since Franklin, Jay, and Jefferson first established a newborn democracy in the family of nations. And the Embassy's activities today presage the work of the future. At Paris, moreover, are now carried on under one roof all the activities in which American Foreign Service officers customarily engage.

Until 1924 two separate offices responsible to the State Department were maintained in Paris: the Embassy, headed by an ambassador, and a Consulate General, presided over by a consul general. In theory the ambassador exercised supervision over the Consulate General in a very nebulous way. In practice, however, the activities of the Embassy and those of the Consulate General—not only in Paris, but in every capital of the world where this duplication of offices existed—were carried on in offices as separate as watertight compartments.

It was as if an American corporation had maintained in every capital two distinct offices in charge of two executives independent in practice and having little more than formal contact. In many capitals the lines of social cleavage between diplomatic and consular officers were such that it was the exception for any intimate social contact to be maintained between the ambassador and his staff and the consul general and his staff. In the old days there were diplomatic officers, bred in old-school-tie traditions, who disdained to receive consular colleagues of their own country socially. It may be imagined how loath they were to lower their dignity so far as to occupy themselves with the plebeian problems of the consular officer. If consular officers were received socially at an Embassy, it was only on those rare occasions, such as the Fourth of July or Washington's Birthday, when the American colony as a whole was entertained.

Obviously this state of affairs did nothing to further the interests of the United States. An effort was made to put an end to the anomalies of such a situation by the amalgamation in 1924 of the diplomatic and consular branches into a single Foreign Service of the United States. It was, however, not until some years later that physical amalgamation of the two offices had been effected in most of the capitals of the world. This occurred in Paris in 1933, when a new building was completed opposite the historic Place de la Concorde. This building houses both the chancery, or offices of the Embassy as distinguished from the ambassador's residence, and the offices of the Consulate General.

Although this fusion brought to an end the duplication of many administrative services which had been common to both the Embassy and the Consulate General, it did not in the long run reduce the total personnel required. The horse-and-buggy era of American diplomacy was passing. As administrative personnel was economized by more efficient organization, greater personnel needs arose for the discharge of the technical functions of the Embassy which were constantly expanding. Today the Embassy staff comprises some six hundred persons, including officers, clerks, guards, messengers, and personnel for all the services—three times the number in 1939 and thirty times the number in 1912, when the staff did not exceed a score. In the year 1912 the warnings of World War I were already evident; yet foreign affairs were one of the least concerns of the United States. Two World Wars have taught us not to neglect the Service whose business is to report such warnings and help to shape the policies which enable us to escape their ominous promise.

VII

AN AMBASSADOR IN ACTION

I T WAS NOT until 1944 that the Paris post—one of the
most distinguished in the American Foreign Service—was
held by a professional career diplomat. In that year Jefferson
Caffery, of Louisiana, was named by President Roosevelt as
Ambassador to France.

Ambassador Caffery had scarcely stepped from the plane
that brought him when a set of curious customs closed around
him as inexorably as a squad of invisible gendarmes. The
protocol of prescribed social ritual attending the entrance of
an officer upon his duties, and his functioning thereafter, is
a relic of a diplomacy whose traditions were established in
the great courts of Europe's monarchs. It is still a factor to
be reckoned with and has some practical use to the experienced
diplomat. It has not been so long, however, since protocol
weighed the Foreign Service officer down like festoons of glit-
tering chains.

Late in 1933 the author prepared a report on the protocol
which the Legation in Cairo found it necessary to observe in
its relations with the Egyptian court, with Egyptians and
British officials, and with the foreign diplomatic corps in

Cairo. The report ran to some fifty pages and contained an elaborate enumeration of the ceremony of calls at stated occasions which necessitated the expenditure by each officer in the Legation of from eight hundred to one thousand visiting cards annually.

Shortly after his arrival in Rumania in 1926, William S. Culbertson was playing golf with his secretary. He had not yet been received formally by the King. The secretary observed the Italian Minister on the golf course, and hastening to overtake him explained that the new American Minister was on the course and that he would like to take this opportunity to present him to His Excellency. The proposal threw the Italian Minister into anguished consternation. Going into a St. Vitus dance of expostulation, the Italian envoy exclaimed, with his arms raised to heaven in horror at the suggestion, that it was quite impossible for the American Minister to be introduced to him as long as the latter had not as yet presented his letter of credence.

I knew an American diplomatic officer, schooled in the old traditions, who, upon arriving at a new post, declined to accept an informal invitation from the minister of finance because the officer had not as yet been presented to the minister for foreign affairs, on whom, in courtesy, the officer considered he should first call in accordance with diplomatic protocol before meeting other officials of the government.

Jules Cambon in his delightful essay on diplomacy remarks that no people are more ceremonious than savages, and suggests that fear may very well have conditioned the development of politeness in its elaborate, ritualistic forms.

In the days before diplomatic protocol had been reduced to generally accepted usage, questions of precedence, and the paying of courtesies which one foreign representative expected of another could easily lead to armed conflict between

[83]

countries. For personal honor, men fought duels at the drop of a hat and nations waged war for no better reason, at times, than the fancied or real slight done their foreign representatives.

At a court ball in London in 1768, the Russian Ambassador, who arrived first, took his place immediately next to the Ambassador of the Emperor of the Holy Roman Empire. The French Ambassador, coming in afterwards, succeeded in climbing over a bench and slipping down between his two colleagues, in order to take the place of precedence to which France laid claim. A duel arose out of the incident, in which the Russian Ambassador was wounded. The explanation offered for the incident was that, although Russia recognized France's claim in general, Russian representatives had orders never to quit a place of precedence they had once occupied.

Today, protocol persists in its most elaborate form at such courts as those of St. James's in London, Abdin Palace in Cairo, and the Shah's court at Teheran, to name but a few examples. It is found in its simplest form, probably, at the courts of Copenhagen and Oslo, and in such republican capitals as Paris and Washington. Yet, there may be recalled the furor created in Washington attending the claim of Mrs. Dolly Gann, sister of Vice-President Curtis, who fought a vigorous verbal battle to endeavor to gain recognition of her right, as the hostess of the Vice-President, to take precedence over the hostesses of foreign ambassadors.

In republican Washington, the State Department, unlike other Foreign Offices, has never succeeded in obtaining authority to define the relative precedence as between various officials of the American Government and the diplomatic corps. The trained diplomat has long since learned that the easiest way to avoid controversy attending this vexed issue is not to invite at the same time those whose relative precedence may be the subject of contention.

Even Washington was not free in the early days from riotous contentions among diplomats over their relative precedence. In a debate in the Senate in 1848, Calhoun declared that within his recollection, swords had been drawn in an antechamber of the White House in a dispute over precedence between the French and English ministers.

Ceremony in Paris today is far from the elaborate protocol surrounding the presentation and functioning of American envoys in the past. Formerly, the ambassador was met at the port of his arrival by the French prefect of the district, and a special railway coach was provided for him. At the station in Paris he was met by a protocol officer of the French Foreign Ministry, members of the staff of the Embassy, and leading members of the American colony.

His first duty was to pay a preliminary call on the French foreign minister, followed by a formal call on the French president. On this latter occasion the ambassador was provided with an elaborate guard of honor to accompany him. The ambassador with his staff—all attired in full evening dress—were received by the president in a strictly formal ceremony.

It was only after the presentation of his letter of credence to the president that the ambassador was considered to have entered into his ambassadorship. This custom persists; an ambassador does not officially assume his post until he has presented his credentials. But a great deal of the tinsel has vanished. Today an ambassador usually arrives by air, calls on the foreign minister and—more formally—on the president, but there is no fanfare of trumpets. Thereafter he settles down to work, hampered by very little social ritual which once ruled the life of an ambassador.

The ambassador and his staff are expected, however, to be

most punctilious about the ceremony of leaving cards. It must be borne in mind that one of the primary duties of an ambassador and his staff is to establish the widest possible contacts; the formality of exchanging cards is one of the accepted means to that end. As in the case of all formalities attending social intercourse it should be done correctly or not at all.

Von Stohrer, when German Minister in Egypt before the war, made an implacable enemy of one of the leading British officials in Cairo by inadvertently sending his own and his wife's visiting cards to the British Resident and his wife, at the Resident's office. The British official ordered that the German's cards be immediately sent back with the message that Lady G. did not have her residence at her husband's office.

A messenger of the American Legation in Bucharest, employing an out-of-date list of government officials, upon whom the minister's cards were to be left for New Year in accordance with a European custom, committed the cardinal error of leaving cards at the home of a former under secretary who had been imprisoned a few days previously. The Rumanian Government took violent umbrage at what it interpreted as an unwarranted interference in internal Rumanian affairs. The American Minister had to explain officially that his cards had been left on the imprisoned under secretary by accident and nothing whatever had been meant by it. Pure mistakes of this kind are only important when people take protocol too seriously. Errors in judgment can lead to serious consequences— as might have been the case had the attempt of the collaborationists to compromise the ambassador (mentioned in a previous chapter) been made on a less experienced officer than Mr. Caffery.

Having made his calls on the foreign minister and the members of the French cabinet, the ambassador calls next on his colleagues—with some of whom he will maintain the closest personal and professional relations. In Paris the American ambassador visits the foreign minister, through whom most of his dealings with the French Government are conducted, several times a week. If important, pressing negotiations are afoot he will be in daily contact with the foreign minister. He has frequent contact with the British and Soviet ambassadors, for negotiations with the French Government which are of common concern to the British and Soviet Governments, have greatly increased in number.

An ambassador is not obliged to call personally on all other ambassadors in the capital at which he is accredited. In Paris some countries, for example Switzerland, are represented only by ministers and it suffices for an ambassador to send cards to diplomats of this rank. However, he calls personally on those with whom he will have frequent official contact and those whom he may have known personally at other capitals during his career. One of the great advantages enjoyed by a career chief of mission over a political appointee is that he finds, at whatever capital he may be stationed, colleagues whom he has previously known, and with whom he is able to enter at once upon a footing of friendly intimacy. Diplomats of other countries are most of them career officers, and the same men may find themselves working together in several capitals. When he came to Paris in 1944, Ambassador Caffery found there four chiefs of mission whom he had known previously.

All Foreign Service officers on arriving at a new post, such as Paris, are expected to adhere to the same ritual of calls as the ambassador, but on their several lower levels of prestige and authority. A new counselor is taken by the ambassador to call on the foreign minister; the counselor calls on the various officials of the Foreign Ministry with whom he will have business to transact. All newly arrived Foreign Service officers—

no matter what their rank—are expected to exchange cards with the members of the staffs of all other embassies and legations of the post. They will find among their colleagues at the Foreign Office, as well as in the embassies and legations, many officers whom they have known previously at former posts. Such previous associations can be of inestimable advantage to the officer in his work.

To a sincere man faced with the crucial problems of foreign affairs in the period following World War II, protocol was little more than a way of getting down to work. Ambassador Caffery's schedule on a typical day reveals how heavy and demanding that work can be.

The first part of the Ambassador's morning was devoted to a review of all important telegrams which had been received during the night, and the reading and signing of all important outgoing correspondence which had been prepared for his signature. There were often twenty or twenty-five outgoing telegrams for the Ambassador's consideration, and again as many incoming telegrams, some requiring action by the Ambassador himself or his personal attention to equip him to give the staff instructions for their initial handling. The time of the Ambassador was so taken up with this essential executive function of his office that he seldom received callers before the middle of the forenoon. Appointments on a typical day were:

11:00   Mr. André Geraud (Pertinax), the well-known French journalist, who wished to discuss a particular phase of Franco-American relations.

11:30   Mr. Frank L. Warrin, International Business Machines, calling to review the French economic and political situation for guidance in planning the future activities of his American company in France.

12:00 Mr. Tanguy-Pringent, French Minister of Agriculture, to discuss means for speeding up American assistance in the revival of French agriculture.

12:30 Mr. Vincent Auriol, President of the Foreign Affairs Committee of the Provisional Assembly of the French Government, for a general exchange of views.

Unless compelled to accept an official or otherwise important luncheon engagement, Mr. Caffery remained at his desk and took advantage of the quiet of the lunch hour to read incoming correspondence and dictate to one of his secretaries.

Between all of his appointments, whether in the forenoon or afternoon, the Ambassador was in constant touch with the principal members of his staff.

The Ambassador's afternoon:

3:00 Meeting of the Co-ordinating Committee for Franco-American Relations.

3:30 Congressman Blank, traveling through Europe inspecting United States Army hospital facilities, who called to pay his respects and discuss his mission.

4:00 Staff meeting attended by the Counselor, the Minister Counselor, and Military and Naval Attachés and some six or eight other officers of the Embassy. The Ambassador reviewed the latest developments in the French political situation and discussed individual problems presented to him by some of the officers.

5:00 Call on Foreign Minister Bidault at his request.

6:30 Reception at the Soviet Embassy to celebrate the anniversary of the October Revolution.

8:15 Dinner for twenty-eight guests at the Embassy residence in honor of the French Minister of the Interior.

It will be observed from the foregoing that a typical day in the life of Ambassador Caffery included all four phases of diplomacy; representation, negotiation, reporting, and the protection of American interests. The information which he gave to the representative of the International Business Machines Corporation comes within the last-named category; much of the time devoted to dictation was spent in making reports to the Department of State on the current French situation; his interview with Foreign Minister Bidault was concerned with current negotiations with the French Government; at the Soviet reception and the dinner for the French Minister of the Interior, Ambassador Caffery was representing the President of the United States.

At the reception of the Soviet Embassy, the Ambassador encountered many of his colleagues and exchanged information and views on the current political and economic situation with some of them. At the dinner he talked at length and at leisure with the French Minister of the Interior, in a manner not often possible in either the Embassy or the French Ministry, where interruptions would have been inevitable.

It is rarely that the contacts of the Ambassador at such functions did not bring him information sufficiently important to telegraph to Washington or incorporate in a longer despatch transmitted by mail.

VIII

THE ADMINISTRATIVE WORK
OF THE EMBASSY

IN 1946 the staff of the Paris Embassy comprised some three hundred persons; officers, clerks, guards, messengers, and others. In 1939, the staff numbered only two hundred; in 1912 (with World War I looming like a thunderhead on the near horizon) the staff numbered only twenty. This phenomenal increase reflects the greater complexity of foreign affairs, and the greater attention paid to them by the United States. It is also an exact measure of the growth of the administrative problems faced by our missions abroad, and the Foreign Service home office.

On the professional level, the most critical administrative problems of a big establishment are the allocation of responsibility and the co-ordination of knowledge and of effort. The evolution of a typical telegram illustrates how co-ordination was achieved in daily operations at the Paris Embassy.

An incoming communication from the State Department requested an appraisal of the effect of franc devaluation on

French exports to the United States. It was routed to an officer of the finance and statistics unit of the economic section who had initial responsibility for such matters, and therefore drafted the reply. However, the advice of several other officers was required. The drafting officer knew whom to consult because the Ambassador had assigned definite responsibilities to each of his subordinates, and had laid down procedures to be followed. Since this matter did not involve policy, it did not have to go to the Ambassador for concurrence; the drafting officer's chief took responsibility. (Communications involving policy always went to the Ambassador. When he himself drafted a communication, it was his practice to consult the interested members of his staff.)

Multiply this telegram by seventy or more, add as many despatches to go by mail and you have a fair sample of a day's professional work in the Paris Embassy in 1946. Many of these communications are mere routine; for example, a telegram requesting authorization of travel by an officer bound for a meeting of the Central Rhine Commission. Some of them require sweat and prayer as well as insight and judgment, for they may mean a vital difference in American loans, or increase the food supplies sent to a population on starvation's edge.

Ambassador Caffery held frequent staff conferences to give overall direction to his staff, guide them in policy matters, and co-ordinate their efforts more closely. These were not held at regular intervals, but at such times as the Ambassador found that there were sufficiently momentous questions or changes to justify them. The conferences were generally attended by the two Counselors, the Military and Naval Attachés, the administrative officer, the three principal political officers, the heads of the various sections, the Press Attaché, and others especially concerned with the topic to be discussed. Ambassador Caffery conferred more informally with members of his staff throughout each working day.

Some chiefs of mission find it helpful to convoke occasional conferences of the entire personnel to stimulate morale or to acquaint the staff with issues of outstanding importance to them. Such conferences are particularly advantageous when a new chief of mission takes charge, or when some major problem affecting the entire staff arises.

Foreign Service establishments vary so much in size and in the conditions under which they must work, that these factors alone make it impossible to standardize organization. For example, the work of the Consulate at Shanghai, which deals with Chinese municipal officials, could not function effectively with the same structure which is most efficient for the Embassy at London, which deals with the British Foreign Office and the Court of St. James's. Moreover, the personnel of each mission should be organized in such a way as to make the most of each man's talent, and compensate for whatever deficiencies exist. In a mission where the chief is inexperienced, the professional officers must be so organized that they can carry on the phases of the work of which he is incapable. An experienced chief such as Ambassador Caffery carries his own lead, and organizes his staff into co-ordinated groups of specialists who become highly competent in their tasks.

Another complication in the organization of missions abroad is the ascendancy of the so-called "technical" functions over executive functions. An ambassador is said to perform *executive* functions when he decides upon the organization of his staff or when he calls a conference. He performs *technical* functions when he confers with the foreign minister, makes a political report to the Department, or lays a wreath beneath the statue of George Washington in Paris on Washington's Birthday.

In analyzing the administrative difficulties in the Foreign Service, Mr. Frank S. Hopkins of the Department of State has written:

There are many reasons why a Foreign Service executive should be interested in the technical functions rather than in those of an executive nature. He is by training a technician—that is, a man who performs the technical functions of a diplomat or consul—rather than an executive. The system of rewards and punishments in the Foreign Service is such that an officer's recognition and advancement depend upon his making a good showing in his reporting, his negotiations, his protection and trade promotional activities and his representational efforts. The Service seldom asks the question, "Is he a good executive?" In fact, promotions to executive positions in the Service are usually made on the basis of a man's technical abilities, without the question of his effectiveness as an executive arising at all. And even when an officer rises to one of the top positions in the Service the question one asks about him is always, "Is he a good Ambassador?" and not "Does he run his Embassy well?"

Mr. Hopkins compares a Foreign Service office with a factory, where the technical functions are performed by the workers at the base of the pyramid while the executive or administrative functions are performed by those at the top. Similarly, in an army, the actual fighting is done by the soldiers, lowest in the organization, while the executive functions are performed by the officers. In an embassy, legation, or consulate, however, the technical functions, namely the work of representation, negotiation, reporting, and protection of American interests, are performed by the officers, that is to say, those at the top of the pyramid. So overwhelming is the work of these technical functions that officers find it difficult to give the requisite amount of time to executive duties.

The staff branch of the Foreign Service was created to provide missions abroad with personnel who devote themselves to executive, rather than to technical, work. They are specialists, and their salaries and ranks are such as to give them appropriate authority.

Although the staff branch had not come into existence during the period here selected as a sample of Foreign Service activities abroad, the anatomy of the Paris Embassy nevertheless illustrates how a good organization works in a large establishment. The functions of personnel differ from time to time and from place to place in detail, rather than in their essential nature.

The work of the Embassy was divided among the following sections: (1) political; (2) administrative; (3) economic; (4) consular; (5) information and cultural relations. Each of these sections was subdivided into units supervised by a section chief. In technical matters the Ambassador gave direct orders to the section chiefs. In executive matters he gave orders through his executive officers. These subordinate administrators in turn provided leadership to those under their direct authority. There was thus a close-linked chain of authority which permitted each decision to be taken at its proper level, and did not burden any responsible officer with unnecessary complications in getting advice, information or authority to proceed.

Most missions and consulates, unless the office is a very small one, center the work of administration in an executive officer. The executive officer, as second in command, takes charge of a mission in the absence of the chief. His title during this period is "Chargé d'Affaires ad interim."

The executive officer confers with the Ambassador at least once, and more often than not, several times a day on matters illustrated by the following episodes. When the head of the consular section was unexpectedly transferred to the

Consulate General at Shanghai, under orders requiring him to leave without waiting the arrival of his replacement, the executive officer worked out a plan for reshuffling the duties of certain officers to fill the gap, and presented his recommendations to the Ambassador. When a Congressional investigating committee was due to arrive, the Ambassador and his executive officer conferred concerning hotel accommodations for the members, and the making of arrangements for them to meet the officials of the French Government with whom they might desire to confer. A dinner and reception was planned for the entire committee, and arrangements were made for certain senior officers of the Embassy to invite them individually to their homes. When the Hotel Crillon, where many of the Embassy personnel were lodged and fed, was about to be "derequisitioned" by the Army, the executive officer made a survey of the situation and presented to the Ambassador recommendations for new arrangements. After conference with the Ambassador, these were put into the form of definite proposals and forwarded to the home office in Washington.

Most of the administrative decisions arising in the course of a day at the Embassy, were taken by the executive officer on his own responsibility. The more important decisions he executed himself. The great burden of execution, however, fell upon his six assistants. These were: a liaison officer who formed the administrative link with the information and cultural relations section; a liaison officer forming the link with the economic section; the chief of the consular section; the administrative services officer; the administrative officer; and the assistant administrative officer. Administrative officers and their assistants are staff branch employees since passage of the Foreign Service Act of 1946. American employees in the administrative units are also staff personnel.

The administrative services officer was a colonel on loan

from the Army to perform emergency services which ended with the return of stable conditions. These services included management of two hotels run by the Embassy for its own personnel and Americans in Paris on business; supervision of a commissary which distributed rations for the hotel messes and to the thousand or more Americans (many of them on official business) who were entirely dependent upon these supplies to maintain their homes.

A large part of the time of the executive officer and his two administrative officers was taken up by visitors. The work of administration and consular activities are to a certain extent interlocked (a fact which was taken into account in framing the Foreign Service Act of 1946, which provides that members of the staff may be commissioned as consuls or vice-consuls). Most of the services which can be rendered to private citizens who call at a Foreign Service establishment, are performed by consular officers.

The seven principal administrative units of the Paris Embassy were under the immediate supervision of the administrative officers: (1) the accounting unit, with a staff of sixteen, met the Embassy's disbursements and accounted for these on the elaborate forms required by the General Accounting Office of the United States; * (2) the code room, with a staff of twenty-six, handled code messages. Messages exchanged between any embassy and its satellite consulates, with missions in other parts of the world, and with Washington are usually so confidential that they must be in code; (3) the mail room and; (4) the file room, with a staff of sixteen, received and classified all incoming mail, registered it, and routed it to the interested officers of the Embassy. Outgoing communications

* To draw his monthly pay and allowances, a Foreign Service officer must fulfill an accounting procedure whose complexity makes the preparation of an income-tax return seem a pleasant interlude. The system dates from the time of Adam and is long overdue for replacement by some simpler procedure.

were assembled in the file room for mailing or transmittal by pouch, and the copies properly filed. If an army can be said to travel on its stomach, a mission can be said to live on its files. Both negotiations, which are conducted through precise written instruments, and reports require constant reference to previous correspondence. Many telegrams and letters of instruction demand immediate action, and instant accessibility to the previous file on the subject is essential to the efficient dispatch of business. From the file room, outgoing mail was delivered to the mail room where it was put into outgoing pouches; (5) the courier service, which is made up of young college graduates carefully selected for their fidelity and sense of responsibility, transported these pouches. The couriers traveled on regular schedules between Paris and Washington, Paris and Madrid, and Paris and other European capitals; (6) the telephone service with twelve operators was another responsibility of the administrative officer; (7) the library, presided over by a trained librarian, contained 7,000 books, a large part of which were in the important Wallace Collection.

In addition to the administrative duties already described, the executive officer and his subordinates are responsible for preparing the seemingly endless reports—more complex than those which harrowed American businessmen during the war —required of its missions abroad by the United States Government.

IX

THE EMBASSY'S
POLITICAL SECTION

AMBASSADOR CAFFERY retained direct authority over the political work, which in many missions is supervised by the counselor in charge of political relations. He himself performed the most responsible part of this phase of the Embassy's activities.

The detailed political work was the responsibility of five Foreign Service officers holding the ranks of first secretary and consul, second secretary and consul, third secretary and vice-consul, and attaché. In addition, the services of the Labor Attaché were actively utilized in the work of the political reporting section.

The political reports of the Embassy kept the Department of State fully informed regarding developments in both internal politics and in the foreign policy of the French Government. Most journalists would not go beyond reporting such developments. The Embassy sought to analyze them all, and to distinguish both short and long term trends by which future developments could be forecast. To attain these objectives it was necessary for the political officers—the Ambassador and his aides in political reporting—to explore and develop the widest possible sources of information among officials and all classes of French society. Such contacts also afforded these officers the opportunity to interpret and explain American foreign policy in general, and American policy towards France in particular.

With the State Department's needs in mind, the political officers followed carefully and promptly reported the decisions taken in cabinet meetings; significant debates in the Assembly; the enactment of important laws and decrees; the activities of political parties; election results both local and national; French relations with other countries as they developed through various treaties and other agreements; French public opinion as reflected in the press and gleaned during the intercourse of members of the Embassy with officials and private individuals; and colonial legislation and policy. Assisting the Embassy in its political reporting were the consular officers stationed in various important French cities. Their reports were reviewed and consolidated by the Embassy and embodied in the over-all reports submitted to Washington.

In addition to the reporting activities of the political section of the Embassy, the officers charged with this work were engaged continually in the work of negotiation. Some of this was merely routine, such as the drafting of various notes to the French Ministry of Foreign Affairs in conformity with instructions from the Department of State and the discharge of the current business of the Embassy. Upon the political section fell also the responsibility of transmitting to the Department copies of notes received from the French Ministry of Foreign Affairs, with appropriate comments and, in many instances, recommendations concerning the action which the Embassy considered desirable.

In addition to the routine business of negotiation the officers of the section were frequently called upon by the Ambassador, along with officers from other sections, to initiate important negotiations with officials of their corresponding rank in the Foreign Ministry.

In the modern world the relations between States have become so intimate that hardly a day passes which does not see some negotiation in process. During a year many volumes of the archives of the Department of State are taken up with those negotiations; here it will suffice to cite, by way of example, but one of the negotiating activities of the Paris Embassy.

On the eve of the war there was concluded between the United States and France a convention on double taxation. One of its purposes was to relieve residents of one country who received income from the other country, from the imposition of taxes by both countries in a manner which might become an intolerable burden. At the time of negotiation the average American tax was twelve per cent on income received from American securities by foreigners residing outside the United States. The French Government agreed in 1939 to reduce its tax rate on such income by 12 per cent. The United States agreed to make appropriate deduction of federal income tax in the case of French nationals residing in the United States.

However, between the years of 1939 and 1945, the rate imposed by the United States Government had increased from twelve per cent to thirty per cent, so that application of the convention failed to accord the relief intended. Accordingly, conversations were opened by the Embassy with the French Foreign and Finance Ministries in an effort to ameliorate the situation pending a revised convention.

As usual in such cases, the negotiations were begun by subordinates. Officers of the economic section of the Embassy met with their colleagues in the Ministry of Finance. At an appropriate moment Ambassador Caffery entered the discussions by taking the matter up in conversations with Foreign Minister Bidault. As a result, the French Government agreed to a more liberal interpretation of the Franco-American double taxation convention of 1939. The tax payable to the French on income from the United States was reduced from forty-one to only eleven per cent. Americans resident in France and French nationals with American investments were both greatly benefitted.

In former times the political work of an Embassy tended to be conducted in a vacuum. Today political, economic, financial, informational and cultural work are so interdependent that the political officers found it necessary to maintain the closest contact with the other sections of the Embassy.

So extensive has been the political reporting of the Paris Embassy that in order to maintain contact with all sections of public opinion, it was found necessary for the Foreign Service officers charged with this work to specialize in particular fields. Under Ambassador Caffery, one officer devoted himself to each of the following geographical divisions of French affairs: the Far East and Eastern Europe; the Near East and Central Europe; and North Africa, where France has important colonial interests. The work of following internal political developments was distributed among these same officers of the political section. One officer specialized in the Left-wing movements, while two others divided between them the different groups within the Socialist, M.R.P., and Right-wing parties—allocation depending upon the personal contacts of each of the officers. The political work was by no means strictly compartmentalized, however. Foreign Service officers from other sections of the Embassy, such as the Counselor and Consul General and the highly experienced First Secretaries were frequently called upon, in the light of their knowledge of Europe and South and Central America, to investigate and report upon French political developments as they might affect those areas, or as the situation in those areas might have some bearing upon French developments of interest to the United States.

Ambassador Caffery's keen interest in the junior members of his staff, and his appreciation of the need to develop their talents, led him to encourage the greatest possible latitude in the reporting of the political section. While all the threads of the work were necessarily kept in his hands, the maximum initiative was encouraged. Instead of waiting for specific instructions from the Ambassador, these officers were accustomed to prepare draft reports on their own initiative. These reports were sent to the Ambassador for his approval. He might decide to forward a particular report to Washington without change; he might suggest some addition or correction; or he might consider it preferable to wait for a few days until the situation had crystallized and the report could be given a more definitive character.

The Ambassador himself often suggested some particular subject for development as a report. The officer so assigned reviewed his product with his colleagues in the political section before submitting it to Mr. Caffery.

In order to keep fully informed of all political developments in their respective fields, the political officers spent at least one hour every morning in reading the numerous Parisian newspapers. In 1946, three of these were of capital importance: *L'Aube, Populaire,* and *L'Humanité,* respectively the official organs of the M.R.P., Socialist, and Communist parties in France. These journals reflected in their morning editorials the official viewpoint of these three major parties on all current problems.

Another important task of the political officers was to review each morning all incoming telegrams from the Department and the immediate drafting of the necessary notes to the Foreign Ministry in accordance with such instructions as the telegrams might contain. Two of the political officers visited the Foreign Ministry almost daily to gather information on the French official attitude towards international questions of interest to the United States. For instance, the closing of the French frontier with Spain might necessitate inquiry by a First Secretary, or even an inquiry of the Foreign Minister by the Ambassador himself. Explanation of the French action was eagerly awaited by the Department of State, for numerous reasons. It could affect the concerted action which the United States, Great Britain, and France had been taking toward the Spanish problem. It might also raise the larger question of the status of security between France and Spain, which was of vital interest to the United States as a world power and member of the Security Organization of the United Nations.

Working in closest contact with the political section of the Embassy was a specialist new to American diplomacy—the Labor Attaché. This position was created in recognition of the importance of the voice of labor in the affairs of the world. The very suggestion that labor should be represented in important missions would have sent shivers down the spines of the diplomats of the old school. One can imagine what Lord Curzon would have thought of the development, or Ambassador Francis who, when a mob crying for justice for Tom Mooney surged around his Embassy in Petrograd in 1915, asked petulantly in a telegram to the Department, "Who is this Tom Mooney about whom the Russian workers are making so much ado?"

The times have passed, if they ever existed in the modern world when diplomats could afford to ignore labor, and derive all their knowledge of the state of public opinion from the smart salons of the capital cities. Dowagers, who once were thoroughly informed of the gossip of courts and inner financial circles, are quite undependable sources today. For out of the laboring element are most likely to come the leaders of future governments. The life and thought of the workers of every country are, therefore, to be observed continually and understood fully.

In no country is labor more influential than in England. It was in recognition of its growing importance that the Embassy in London requested in 1942 the assignment of a labor specialist. On the recommendation of Mr. Isador Lubin, Mr. Sam Berger was assigned to London as the first Labor Attaché of the Department of State abroad.

The value of the work performed by Mr. Berger led the Department of State to expand the service and to make it general in character. By 1946, twenty labor attachés had been appointed to American diplomatic missions, twelve of them in Europe and eight in South and Central America.

In France the principal task of the Labor Attaché is to keep informed of the viewpoints and activities of organized labor by close contact with its leaders, and to keep the Department of State advised. All significant developments in the field of labor are reported.

In France, as is well known, organized labor has been a powerful force for many years. With the liberation, the power of French labor increased many fold. The French Government, therefore, utilizes advisory councils of organized labor, along with similar councils of organized employers, when considering the adoption of important legislation or any new measure affecting labor.

The appointment of labor attachés to the staffs of the British and French Embassies was at first regarded with some reserve by organized labor in France. However, once it came to be understood that through the Labor Attaché, French labor had an opportunity to make known its viewpoint to these governments which contributed substantially to French reconstruction—the co-operation of French labor with the Labor Attaché became increasingly cordial.

French labor, indeed, became so impressed with the value of such an officer, that the French Confederation of Labor petitioned the government to appoint French labor attachés abroad. In the Constituent Assembly on January 17, 1946, Mr. Paul Rivet, Socialist Deputy, said: "Our country must do what the English and the Americans have already done; we must send abroad, as the French Confederation of Labor asks, men familiar with the labor movement and with labor questions."

Another Deputy, M. Gazier, commenting on the same proposal, declared: "There are already labor attachés in Paris at the British and American Embassies; they render the greatest service to their countries in reporting the real views of labor in France. An ambassador is not merely a contact with the technicians of diplomacy or with particular social groups; he is also a link with the people to whom he is accredited."

X

THE EMBASSY'S
CONSULAR SECTION

I N THE PERIOD we are considering as a representative
sample of Embassy activities, the United States maintained
consular establishments at Marseilles, Lyons, Nice, Le Havre,
Bordeaux, Cherbourg, and Strasbourg; others were to be added
when circumstances were proper. All of these were under the
supervision of the consular section of the Embassy at Paris.
This arrangement is typical of countries where, as in France,
the political capital is also the chief commercial and financial
city. In countries where the political capital is not the economic nerve-center, the consular headquarters may be separate from the Embassy. In the United States, for example, the
principal British consulate is in New York City. The American
Consulate General at Barcelona supervises our consular offices
in Spain—the consular section of the Embassy at Madrid being
small, with relatively minor consular duties to perform. Because of its importance and the great variety of its task, the
work of the consular section of the Paris Embassy embraces
almost the full range of consular activities, and provides as
good an example as can be found.

[107]

The consular officer maintains much more intimate touch with the lives of Americans abroad than does the diplomatic officer. The latter's principal job is to execute *policy*, whereas the former is responsible for executing *laws*—both those which Americans, though far from home, must still obey, and the laws which foreigners must obey when they come to, or do business with, the United States. Whereas the diplomatic officer is usually called upon to protect the larger interests of the United States, the consular officer looks out for the property and welfare of individuals, and often must act as their representative.

It is the consular officer to whom the American abroad comes if distress overtakes him: who is witness to his marriage, registers the birth of his children, and arranges his affairs when he dies abroad.

The consular officer combines the functions of the secretary of a Chamber of Commerce, a justice of the peace, a notary public, a commissioner of immigration and naturalization, and a Veterans Administration official. Outside the capital he must be some part of a mayor, for he is, officially speaking, the principal American citizen of the community. At this point the consular officer's duties merge with those of the diplomat; for he must represent the United States on ceremonial occasions. He must also perform outpost duty in the work of reporting and negotiation.

To carry on this variety of duties, the consular officer must be equipped with knowledge which would tax any man's learning ability. He must be thoroughly versed in the citizenship and immigration laws of the United States; with our extensive legislation on the peculiar rights of seamen, and with the multitudinous functions he is authorized to perform in behalf of American shipping. He must know where to turn to find instantly the laws of each of the forty-eight states regulating notarial services. He must know the laws and customs of the community in which he is stationed, and understand how to get along with both the people and the officials. Toward Americans he should show the sympathy and understanding of a chaplain, and at all times command their co-operation and respect.

In a small consulate, many of the services are performed under the direct supervision of a single officer. But in Paris the great volume of work must be broken down into units specializing in one, or at the most, a few services. In the postwar period we are here describing, the chaotic conditions in Europe, and the changed relationships between nations, threw unusually heavy burdens upon the consular officers. They faced unusual problems—such as the shuffling hordes of displaced persons—and often performed their work under especially trying conditions. Nevertheless, the differences between the traditional work of consular officers and their activities during the critical times of reconstruction, was largely fantastic expansion and pressure, rather than difference in kind. The consular units of the Paris Embassy did not substantially change their nature, but rose to the occasion by adding what personnel could be employed and working harder and with more resolution than ever before.

The visa unit of fifteen persons, performed the consular service's traditional functions as an outpost of the American immigration service. Our laws require consular officers to examine each applicant for admission to the United States, verify the documents which he must submit, fill out the proper forms, and issue the visa. The number of French nationals (and those of every other country) permitted to enter the United States as permanent residents, is limited to a definite quota, from which the wives of American citizens, and certain other categories of emigrants are excepted. The law bars bigamists, persons convicted of crimes, persons advocating the overthrow of the government by force or violence, believers in polygamy, and some other undesirables.

The law is so explicit that consular officers have very little discretion as to who shall be granted a visa. For example, under the present law, which permits 3,086 French nationals to enter the United States each year, a person born in France of a Syrian mother and a Portuguese father must be considered French and admitted under the quota, if he presents the proper documents. The explicitness of the law makes the examination of immigrants and the issuing of visas a fairly routine matter most of the time. But occasionally a case comes up which taxes the ingenuity and discretion of the consular officer and justifies the rigorous investigations made by the special services of the Embassy. The history of Marie, the pretty collaborationist, is illuminating.

Marie applied to the consular section of the Embassy for a visa to permit her to proceed to the United States as the wife of an American citizen whom she had married in 1945. As a result of the customary check which the special services of the Embassy make, some highly informative facts were revealed concerning Marie, which she would have been the last to vouchsafe either to the Embassy or to her unsuspecting American soldier husband.

It appeared that Marie was born in the Department of the Seine and Marne. During the occupation of France she was in constant touch with the Germans. She was so far attached to the Germans that, even when Allied troops swept through France, Marie accompanied a group of German soldiers in their retreat as far as Germany. Subsequently she succeeded, in the confusion of the surrender, in slipping back into France and in losing herself in Paris.

Marie's activities had been too well known in her community for her to escape the hand of justice. A warrant of arrest was issued against her on March 26, 1945. She was charged with activities prejudicial to the security of the state. In the absence of any trace of her in her home town, Melun, or any knowledge of her whereabouts, Marie was sentenced "in absentia" to twenty years' hard labor, twenty years' exile from the Department of the Seine and Marne, confiscation of all her property, and national indignity.

Marie might have escaped justice forever in this life, had she not overplayed her hand. In Paris she found an American gullible enough to believe the story she told of her patriotic devotion to France and the Allied cause. She was not content to have him for a friend; she saw in marriage with him the chance to escape from France, where she might be recognized at any time by her former acquaintances and delivered over to justice.

When Marie applied to the Embassy for documentation in connection with the issuance to her of a visa, she gave her name and her Paris address. The Embassy's inquiries revealed the previous indictment and conviction. Consequently, notwithstanding the Act of December 28, 1945 admitting GI wives without visas, she was found ineligible to enter the United States, under Section 3 of the Immigration Act of 1917, which bars persons convicted of crime.

When the French authorities were informed of Marie's whereabouts in Paris, she was promptly arrested and at this writing is languishing in prison.

France has always been the mecca for less fortunate Europeans, who come there in the hope of eventually reaching the United States. As many as France would permit sought refuge after the Second World War. They are patient, and pressure on the visa unit of the Embassy will be heavy for many years to come.

The passport and citizenship unit of the Embassy looks into the cases of persons who—for one reason or another—are without the American passports to which they claim to be entitled. This is part of the normal work of the Embassy, but in the confused period following the Second World War it grew very heavy. In the year 1945, the Embassy received some 3,000 applications and issued almost 2,000 passports. Many of these were issued to American soldiers demobilized in Europe and wishing to reside in France. Among the cases were those of two hundred "displaced persons" of American citizenship who had been swept into France from the U.S.S.R., Lithuania, Poland, and half a dozen other countries of Europe. People of many languages and backgrounds brought forward complex claims —though some legitimate—to the citizenship that would get them to a land where there was enough to eat. The Embassy also received applications for registration from the United States citizens who had remained in France throughout the war.

The ways in which citizenship is established are very definitely specified by law; the consular officer's area of interpretation is small, and the more difficult cases are referred to the Department of State. The applicant may, as a last resort, appeal to United States Courts. Nevertheless, the Embassy's passport and citizenship unit has knotty problems. Shifting allegiance and wanderings over half of Europe make tangles that are very hard to unravel, and applicants often complicate matters by lying to make their claims seem more valid.

A young boy appeared before the officer in charge of the citizenship unit of the Embassy in 1945, to make application for an American passport. He claimed that he had been born in Brooklyn, taken to Poland by his father when of a tender age, and that during the war he had been sent to Germany to do forced labor on a farm. The officer asked him in German where he had been living in Germany. He stared dumbly at her inquiry. She then asked him in English to tell her the German words for cow and horse. When he was unable to answer satisfactorily, she sent for a Polish interpreter and asked him to tell the boy to come out with the truth.

The boy confessed that his story was made out of whole cloth—except for his American birth. At the outbreak of war he had been inducted into the Soviet Army and he was afraid to confess the truth for fear that it would keep him from returning to the United States. Although he denied that he had taken an oath of allegiance to the Soviet Union, the Department of State to which the case was referred, held that the boy had in fact expatriated himself. It was further ruled that a passport could be issued to him upon application for the resumption of citizenship under the Act of April 2, 1942, which provides that those who lost their American citizenship in performing military service in an allied army, may recover it.

An American citizen may use foreign passports and foreign identity cards; he may openly side with the enemy and support him in his speech; he may engage in the most inimical activities against the United States Government, even in time of war —and still remain an American citizen. American protection can be withheld administratively while he is abroad. But the law draws the line only when an American citizen takes an oath of allegiance or becomes formally naturalized as a citizen or subject of another country. Unless an American has formally changed his allegiance, the Department of State is obliged to issue a passport for his return to the United States if he requests it.

Of the 1,600 Americans who remained in France throughout the war, there were a few notorious collaborationists. Except for a few who had changed allegiance under oath, the Embassy was obliged to permit the return of these people, who thus escaped the penalty of their devotion to the enemy which would surely have overtaken them had they remained in France. This is a good example of the fact that—whatever his own feelings may be—the Foreign Service officer must execute laws and policies made by the elected representatives of the American people.

In addition to registering American citizens, and issuing new passports, this unit carried on the normal, day-to-day work of renewing, validating, and amending passports in current use. Just before the First World War, a traveler could go anywhere in Europe without a passport—so long as he did not cross the frontiers of Russia or Turkey. But war and threats of war have made all governments, including our own, highly suspicious of travelers. Whereas passports were, and may some day be again, made valid for travel in all countries, they are at present restricted to stated areas. Other definite limitations have been placed upon their use. Moreover, it was not enough, during the postwar period, to have a visa to enter; one had also to obtain an exit permit. In one single day of 1945, the Paris Embassy assisted sixty-eight American citizens to get exit permits.

These restrictions required much additional paper work, which meant more man hours and extra expense both for the traveler and the government services. It is difficult to find any one who has gained any advantage from these hampering regulations, except perhaps the paper manufacturers.

As the fingers of the American Government's long arm, Foreign Service officers are frequently called upon to perform special services, required by unusual circumstances and likely to be discontinued when circumstances change. A typical job of this sort was the naturalization of members of our armed forces who were candidates for citizenship. Ordinarily, the Immigration and the Naturalization Service of the Department of Justice examines applicants for citizenship. But before the end of the Second World War, almost one hundred members of the Foreign Service had been appointed special examiners, so that the troops overseas could be naturalized without delay.

Their work often took these Foreign Service officers into the front lines. One vice-consul was decorated for bravery displayed in the course of his naturalization work. Another vice-consul traveled more than 20,000 miles to make citizens of over 1,800 "foreigners" in the Army of the United States. Here is his firsthand account of one of these missions:

At the various divisions and corps near the front the men were brought directly to us from their tanks which were firing, their squads which were fighting, right from the fox holes, and from medical units on the firing line. Very seldom was there electric light and often we finished our work by lamp or candlelight, and the oath was read by aid of an electric flashlight. . . .

The men were all splendid soldiers, all with excellent records, many with citations and decorations, and I am sure that they appreciate to the fullest extent the high privilege of American citizenship and that they will make fine citizens. . . . One evening an officer and a soldier came in just as we were preparing to move on to another division. It was snowing and raining and a cold wind was blowing. They had been many hours on the way and had only found us with difficulty. The soldier was very tired, almost exhausted; they were both unshaven, soiled, stained, and dirty, and the soldier stood there in a miserable dirty room in a miserable little house, in a tiny, partly wrecked village in Belgium, and I read the oath to him by candlelight. I took his hand to congratulate him and he broke down completely. "I am sorry, sir. I apologize. I just couldn't help it—thought I never would get to be an American citizen up here. Now at last I am a citizen and those other guys will never be able to call me a foreigner again." A strong handclasp and he was gone off to duty at the front. Before

I naturalized him I read in his records that he had been decorated
for extraordinary bravery in action during the battle of Huertgen
Forest.

The young woman who was consular officer in charge of the
whereabouts, welfare, repatriation, and miscellaneous correspondence unit just after World War II, kept on her desk the
picture of a tiny Polish girl. The child was named Irenka, and
her picture was a sort of talisman against discouragement and
impatience with the demands of hundreds of visitors clamor-
ing for help. For Irenka's is the story of a minor miracle. Early
in the occupation her parents and close relatives—a family of
fifteen altogether—were herded with other Jewish people into
"Ghetto A" at Kobryn. Irenka's father was a physician, and
partly because he had given them medical care and partly out
of the kindness of their hearts, a gentile family named Slawin
supplied them with vegetables and milk. They passed these
supplies through a tunnel that came up into the ghetto
garden.

"One night the Germans murdered everyone in Ghetto B,"
wrote Anatol Slawin in a letter to Irenka's American relatives.
"Inda sent us a heartbreaking, tear-stained letter begging us
to take her youngest daughter, Irenka, aged one and a half
years, saying that she would be able to take care of the other
child and save herself. You, no doubt, will understand what a
momentous decision that was for us: on the one hand, the begging of a mother to save her child—could it be refused? And on
the other, the threat of the Germans to kill us and our children
for hiding a Jewish child.

"We hesitated. My wife cried all day. . . . So it happened
that my wife when it grew dark went to the fence surrounding
the ghetto. Irenka, whom the doctor had put to sleep, was
handed to her. . . . A few days later the Germans killed everyone in Ghetto A. It is believed your brother administered

[116]

poison to the whole family and that, securing arms, he fought the Germans. . . ."

Anatol Slawin's letter reached Irenka's uncle when he was serving as a medical officer with the American forces at Le Havre. With the help of the Embassy, he located Irenka, had her brought to Paris and then sent to his home in the United States.

The facilities of the United States Government are always at the disposal of American citizens anxious for word concerning the whereabouts and welfare of their kin abroad. In normal times this phase of consular work can be humdrum, but during the post-war period there was hardly a day the Paris Embassy was not crowded with dramatic incidents. The wholesale displacement of persons throughout Europe, the complete absence of communication facilities during the war, brought a flood tide of inquiries regarding the whereabouts and welfare of American citizens, alien near relatives of persons domiciled in the United States, and of persons in the United States Army.

Many of the "whereabouts" problems which the Embassy encountered during this period were similar to those of social agencies in the United States. Each day several letters came in from French girls inquiring for the whereabouts of American soldiers. Some of these girls had been promised marriage; many had become mothers and had lost track of the fathers of their children. Hundreds of letters were received from French patriots eager to learn what had become of American fliers whom they had befriended after they had bailed out over occupied territory. The Embassy found out all it could; answered each of the letters, and dealt with each of the pressing problems as tactfully and patiently as it was able to do.

The war also forced on the Embassy the problems of repatriating American citizens stranded abroad. In normal times the government does not assume this burden, in the absence of any appropriation therefor from Congress. Before the war pressing appeals were made to American citizens to return to their homeland before the storm broke above their heads. Thousands heeded the warning but there were many so rooted in the homes they had made abroad that they preferred to remain behind. With the liberation of France, many of these were repatriated. Many were destitute. Those without funds were supplied sufficient money by the Embassy for their living expenses, and were assisted with packages of food and other necessities by American relief agencies working in close concert with the consular section of the Embassy.

The volume of miscellaneous correspondence handled by the consular section swelled until it became almost a major problem in itself. With millions of American soldiers in France, it was inevitable that some citizens would write in to complain about their behavior. The creation of good will toward the United States is one of the prime objectives of American Foreign Service officers. To have ignored such correspondence would have caused the wounds occasioned by thoughtless and irresponsible soldiers to rankle deeper. Accordingly, every letter received by the Embassy, unless from an obvious crank, was answered with great care in the hope of turning irritation into friendship.

Unlike the British foreign service, American Foreign Service officers are not authorized to perform marriages in which one or both of the parties are American citizens. However, they may act as witnesses and are authorized to issue a certificate to that effect. Some Americans living abroad have an exaggerated conception of the importance of a consular officer's presence at a marriage ceremony—as is attested by the words of a Protestant missionary in China officiating at a marriage several years ago: "In the presence of Almighty God and of

Vice-Consul Walter A. Adams, I now pronounce you man and wife."

The anxiety of many Americans to be married in an embassy is no doubt occasioned by the mistaken conception that to be joined on ground officially American and in the presence of American officers gives American validity to the marriage. Marriages performed abroad, however, have no greater validity than that given them by the local law of the country. American Foreign Service officers may permit, within their discretion, marriages to be performed between American citizens on the official premises of the mission or consulate, but this does not give any special sanction to the marriage.

In peacetime it is the duty of consular officers to report the demise of American citizens who die in their districts, and to take charge of and conserve the estates of those without executors and agents available locally. As Paris has long been the mecca of the American tourist, the care of estates was no small part of the "estates, veterans, and selective service registration unit." This unit also performed a host of duties on behalf of veterans of both world wars. In fact, the Embassy became a small Veterans Administration for ex-servicemen who elected to make their homes in France. Veterans' benefits are applicable abroad and the problems connected with them were even more difficult to resolve than in the United States.

Consular officers are charged under the law with the issuance to exporters of invoices covering a wide range of merchandise destined for shipment to the United States. This work is tedious because of its extremely technical character and is usually given, along with other routine duties such as performance of notarial services, to the fledgling Foreign Service officer at a post.

The procedure in connection with notarial services is sometimes heartbreaking in its protraction. Suppose an American citizen or a French national lives in a small community in France not easily accessible to a consulate. He executes before a French notary in a village an important document which is to be used as evidence in the United States. The notary's signature must be forwarded to the prefecture for authentication. When the document is returned, it must be forwarded to the Ministry of the Interior for authentication of the prefect's signature, and then to the Ministry of Foreign Affairs for authentication of the signature of the Minister of the Interior. Only then is it in order for authentication by the American Embassy. If one is not bedridden and can afford a long journey and the affair does not require a French notary, it is more convenient to make a hundred-mile trip to the nearest American consulate and obtain the authentication direct. For the notarial seal and signature of consular officers are alone recognized in American courts as valid evidence from abroad.

The notarial work in Paris, which formerly was confined largely to income-tax declarations, patent applications, immigration visa petitioners, and the accompanying affidavits of support, became more diversified after the Second World War. Callers of almost every nationality clamored constantly for the legalization of documents of every description, their consuming desire being to obtain the bright red seal of the Embassy to give *an imposing air*. The most careful scrutiny of the legitimate purpose of the document was necessary.

It is difficult to realize the misuse to which a document bearing the seal of a consular officer may be put.

Some years ago an American citizen, approaching the age of thirty, appeared in Cairo. His engaging personality quickly gained him the confidence of both the local American and Egyptian communities. He readily found employment and was soon occupying a post of considerable confidence in a local commercial enterprise. A year or more having passed and his position in Cairo being securely established, he appeared at the American Consulate with a formidable appearing legal document. This purported to be a copy of the will of his father, and went into most specific detail regarding bequests to the son of several hundred thousand dollars, to which he was to fall heir at the age of thirty. The will had ostensibly been entered in a court in Pennsylvania, a court which, as it was afterwards discovered, was nonexistent. The Consulate, being empowered to authenticate only the seal and signature of the Secretary of State among American officials, would obviously have refused to authenticate the seal and signature of the court in Pennsylvania.

The young man was sufficiently mature and well-informed not to request the performance of what he knew to be an impossible service. He therefore limited his request to the legalization of his own signature, a service which the officer could not withhold unless he had reason to believe the legalization, accompanied by the seal and signature of the consul, was to be put to improper use.

Having obtained on the copy of the will a bright red seal of the United States and the signature of the consul attesting to the fact that the applicant had appeared personally before him and had sworn that the copy was a true one—the youthful rogue submitted it to certain influential and rich Egyptians as American Government confirmation of the facts set forth in the will and also its genuineness. On the strength thereof a hundred thousand dollars was advanced him with no other security than an assignment of his rights under the fictitious will. A short while later the impostor decamped in the night from Cairo and nothing has ever been heard or seen of him since.

Paris being inland, shipping services which in a port such as Marseilles or Naples assume major importance in consular work, are relatively unimportant in the consular section of the Embassy. Seamen, however, frequently come to Paris for sight-seeing purposes and overstay their leaves. They are often without funds and have to be taken care of while arrangements are made to return them to their own or other ships.

The property protection unit of the Embassy is charged with the protection of private and industrial American property situated in the Paris district. With the extraordinary conditions obtaining in France upon the reopening of the Embassy in 1944, one of the most urgent tasks faced by this unit was to prevent the requisition of American apartments, dwellings, and commercial premises, and otherwise protect American interests. The Franco-American Consular Convention extends no greater rights to American citizens in respect of real and personal property than those enjoyed by French citizens. The officers charged with these duties were, therefore, limited—when they dealt with French authorities—to an informal friendly approach. With a view to extending over American holdings such protection as was available, the Embassy issued no less than 5,000 certificates attesting American ownership, to be posted on the properties themselves.

Moreover, an informal agreement was reached with the French authorities, whereby American property was requisitioned only in urgent circumstances. It was also agreed that requisition would be applied only after prior reference to the Embassy. The result was to spare from requisition innumerable apartments and dwellings belonging to American citizens.

The property protection work of the Embassy extended to various other problems such as claims of American citizens for damages resulting from bombings, lootings, and other war hazards, seeking the recovery of spoliated Jewish property belonging to Americans, obtaining indemnities for requisitioned premises, and recovering property sequestered under Vichy or German order.

In describing the work of the consular section of the Embassy in Paris it has been possible to touch upon only major functions which the work of the consular officer entails. These duties are so many and so varied that literally hundreds of pages of the Foreign Service Regulations of the United States are taken up with their definition and with the rules to be observed in their execution. Nor is it sufficient merely to follow the rules. The Honorable Ely E. Palmer, in November, 1946, Minister to Afghanistan, once laid down to one of his subordinates in the Consulate General at Bucharest an admirable precept which all Foreign Service officers ought to bear in mind: "When you search the regulations, do not look for an excuse for not acceding to the request of an American citizen; the regulations can be turned easily enough with that in view. Look to the regulations, rather, for a means to be of service."

XI

THE EMBASSY'S
ECONOMIC SECTION

THE ECONOMIC WORK of the Embassy is a reflection
of a mature sense of economic interdependence. The
notion that we can live in a self-enclosed economy, and build
up a prosperous United States by spurring exports and ignor-
ing the economic state of other countries is outmoded. During
the past quarter century we have learned the billion dollar
lesson; no nation can live in a state of economic or political
seclusion; the fortunes of each are bound up with the fortunes
of all. With states as with individuals, "there are no islands any
more."

Today the trade promotion of our Foreign Service officers
abroad—which was once almost the sole assignment in this field
—is only one phase of their economic work. The objective is no
longer the ensuring of a "favorable balance of trade," but
economic prosperity around the entire globe.

In 1944, in recognition of the inseparability of economic
from political work, the Department of State appointed to our
more important missions, minister counselors for economic

affairs equivalent in rank to the minister counselors for political affairs. The equivalence of rank should be particularly noted, since it emphasizes the degree of importance attached today and for the future to the close integration of our political and economic foreign relations, each reacting upon the other and each being indissoluble from the other. The first Minister Counselor for Economic Affairs was Mr. Harry C. Hawkins appointed to London.

For the discharge of the multifarious activities devolving upon the Paris Embassy's economic speculation, the Economic Counselor had working under him on January 1, 1946, no less than twenty-nine officers and thirty clerical assistants. By reason of the diversity of its duties, the economic section was broken up into eight units: (1) wartime and emergency economic problems; (2) civil aviation; (3) telecommunications; (4) commercial; (5) finance and statistics; (6) agricultural; (7) petroleum; (8) commercial policy.

The work of the economic counselor falls into two broad categories: (1) administrative and supervisory; (2) technical. During the immediate postwar period the position was so new and conditions were so extraordinary that it is hard to say whether his work and organizational position will remain typical.

As one of the principal links in the Embassy's internal network of communication and authority, the Minister Counselor for Economic Affairs attended the staff conferences of the Ambassador and kept abreast of all important political developments. As Mr. Merchant, the Economic Counselor in Paris, has observed: "Economics and politics can no more be separated than the white from the red corpuscles in the blood." The Economic Counselor in turn kept the Ambassador informed of all the economic developments which affected the political situation in France, and all that seemed of particular importance to American interests. In order to maintain fluid contact, Mr. Merchant invited the officer who had (under the Ambassador) general direction of political affairs, to the economic staff conference when a political crisis arose. For example, at the time of the resignation of General de Gaulle, an officer of the political section spent half an hour reviewing the political crisis which had arisen over the week end and gave his prognostications of the probable course of events. The review went much deeper than the newspaper accounts because this political officer thoroughly understood both the main trends and small crosscurrents which underlay the visible events.

The economic staff conferences were ordinarily used to discuss problems and plan operations. For example, a telegram was received from the State Department requesting an encyclopedic answer on the current French economic situation. Questions were asked which no French ministry could answer. After the views of the staff were heard, the task of drafting a reply was entrusted to a committee of the three staff members most intimately acquainted with the subject.

The Economic Counselor's administrative work included, in addition to the staff conferences and liaison with other sections of the Embassy, review of all outgoing telegrams, airgrams, and despatches touching upon matters of policy. He also kept in close touch with the economic activities of American consulates in France, and of those in nearby countries whose work affected his own. To keep abreast of the economic activities of American consulates in France, the Economic Counselor made an eight-day trip in 1945 to establish personal relations with the officers and to learn how the Embassy could contribute to making their economic reporting more effective. He spent three days in Brussels meeting with economic counselors of the American missions to Great Britain, Belgium, and the Netherlands on common problems, and two days at the

Embassy in London conferring on economic problems common to both that Embassy and his own.

First in the field of technical functions came the Economic Counselor's contacts with French officials; the Finance Minister, the Minister of National Economy, the Minister of Food and Agriculture, the Governor of the Bank of France, the Economic Director of the ·Foreign Office, the High Commissioner for National Planning, and many other subordinate but by no means less important officials. The main purpose in maintaining these contacts was to understand France's economic policies as they developed and preserve good working relationships.

Economic policy is made by those outside as well as inside the government. Contact was therefore maintained with leading French businessmen, bankers, and labor leaders. In order to keep up with practical problems of American business interests in France, the Economic Counselor was in close and constant touch with leading members of the local American business community. Economic relations between the United States, the United Kingdom, and Canada were very intimate during this period and the Economic Counselors of the Paris missions of these three countries saw a great deal of one another.

Let it not be thought that the economic counselor's technical functions end here. During the postwar period, inter-nation boards and other organizations played an important part in the economic life of ravaged countries. For example, the Office of the Foreign Liquidation Commission, having jurisdiction over all of Europe, had headquarters in Paris. The Economic Counselor was the point of contact for the Embassy with the Commissioner of that Office on matters of broad economic-political policy throughout western, northern, and southern Europe. He was also the connecting link of the Embassy with the American representative in London on the European Coal Organization, the European Central Inland Transportation Organization, and the Emergency Economic Committee for Europe, on all of which bodies the French Government was represented.

Another technical responsibility, extracurricular in character and heavy in the burden of work imposed, which devolved upon the Economic Counselor in Paris was serving as United States representative on the Central Rhine Commission. The Commission was set up by the Congress of Vienna in 1815 and its status reaffirmed by the Convention of Mannheim of 1869 and Treaty of Versailles of 1919. It is now composed of representatives of the United States, United Kingdom, France, Belgium, the Netherlands, and Switzerland, and of the western allied occupying authorities as trustees for Germany. Its principal responsibility is to maintain the Rhine as an international waterway.

The economic counselor must work with the local American press, and he confers with many visitors in line of duty. When traveling American senators and representatives desire to be enlightened on the economy of France and the advisability of an American loan, the economic counselor's knowledge is at their disposal. He must serve such diverse visitors as a former American Government official, now a coal operator, who desires to inspect personally the French coal mines in Pas-de-Calais, an American woman lecturer with a hungry notebook, the principal Treasury representative from a neighboring post on his way to Washington, a consular officer from Bordeaux in Paris on leave, a mission from the United States on the coal problems of France, and a Frenchman with a letter of introduction from a high government official who wishes to be assisted in obtaining the French agency for a new American automobile company.

The work of the special wartime economic unit of the economic section of the Embassy was largely devoted during the reconstruction period to those interests of the Embassy concerning the disposal of surplus property, liquidating the remains of a few Lend-Lease transactions which were handled in the field, and problems of ship scheduling for the transportation of scarce supplies to Europe, and aiding in the solution of colonial economic problems. Though most of this work grew out of the war and had an emergency character, it is likely to affect the future of both France and the United States, and thus become intertwined with the permanent activities of the Foreign Service. Both major and minor problems were solved —whenever possible—with the intent to work permanent improvement. One typical minor problem was the disposal of surplus property on a "barter" basis. The Embassy proposed to the French Government that the latter make over to the American Government real estate in Paris and other cities in France needed for Foreign Service establishments in part payment of the surplus property placed at the disposal of the French authorities.

A revealing example of the constructive long-range planning brought to bear by the wartime and emergency economic problems unit of the Embassy, is the proposal for large-scale development by the French of timber resources on the Ivory Coast, Cameroons, and Gabon. The example illustrates the fact that our economic experts no longer confine themselves to the stimulation of the flow of exports from the United States. In this instance the long view led them to discover a means by which French economy might be resuscitated and helped to play its part in general world recovery.

Officials of the Embassy and the Department of Commerce, thinking not only of France, but also of the world-wide shortage of timber, became interested in the French Colonies in

Africa. They concluded after appropriate study that, if modern forestry methods were used, the Ivory Coast, Cameroons, and Gabon could supply all the needs of France for most types of wood, and could export enough to foreign countries to meet the cost of the equipment needed for the development. The suggestion to this effect was made to the French authorities interested in colonial questions. It is expected that the initiative thus taken will ultimately prove of economic benefit to the United States, France, and the natives of the territories concerned.

The Second World War ushered in, or rather precipitated, the Air Age. Anticipating the unprecedented development which the war's end would bring to civil air transport, the State Department in 1944 assigned four civil air attachés to missions abroad where civil aviation problems were of actual or potential importance. Mr. Livingston Satterthwaite, assigned to London, was the first. Mr. Howard B. Railey assigned to the Embassy in Paris was given jurisdiction also over aviation matters in Belgium and Luxembourg.

The civil air attaché follows all phases of civil aviation in the countries of his assignment. His special interests are the operation and development of airlines, the negotiation of international arrangements for air transport and air navigation, the use of airports and the foreign market for American aircraft. He makes periodic reports upon these activities.

During the reconstruction period, most of the air attaché's time was taken up with negotiations for individual air transport agreements between the United States and France, Belgium, and Luxembourg.

American interest in such an agreement centered mainly upon what has become known as the "fifth freedom" of the air; the right of international air carriers to pick up international traffic between the intermediate points on their routes, a principle which Great Britain was most insistent in contesting. If this right were granted, a carrier operating between New York, let us say, and Karachi and passing through Paris, would be able to carry passengers and freight between Paris and Cairo, and thus make fully efficient use of its equipment and facilities. This right was finally embodied in the provisional Air Transport Agreement between the United States and France, signed in Paris on December 29, 1945. The two countries granted each other reciprocally the "fifth freedom" of the air.

To bring about this agreement, the Civil Air Attaché worked assiduously to win over those important French officials whose views might determine French air policy. This is a good example of the accomplishments of these Foreign Service specialists who are charged with advancing American air interests in all quarters of the globe.

The growth of telecommunications in both importance and complexity, kept step with the development of air transport. And in 1945 the Department of State determined to appoint to key diplomatic missions specialists capable of dealing with this problem in the field, on behalf of both the Department of State and other government agencies. Telecommunications attachés were assigned in each of the following six regions of the world: Central America, South America, Western Europe, Eastern Europe, the Near East, and the Far East. These attachés are available to the various missions in their respective regions for consultation on telecommunications problems as they arise.

The first such Attaché, Mr. John Plakiar, was assigned to the Paris Embassy and made responsible for telecommunications in Western Europe. His field embraced the telephone, oceanic cables, wireless telegraph, wireless telephone, broadcasting, facsimile telephoto, and television.

International co-operation in telecommunications may be said to date from the establishment of the International Telegraph Union in 1865. This was one of the earliest organs of international collaboration. The telegraph had only recently been introduced and the nations of the world, living in their "splendid" isolation, took—in making this agreement—a first notable step in adjusting themselves to the diminution of space which has contributed so much to making the world one—economically speaking.

The basic agreement in telecommunications is the Madrid Convention of 1932, as revised in Cairo in 1938. The United States is a signatory to that convention and the radio regulations thereunder, but not to the telephone and telegraph regulations.

Communications facilities are one of war's first casualties. During the Second World War, great oceanic cables were cut, radio transmitters destroyed, land lines severed, and local installations were attacked and destroyed. When armies moved into such stricken areas, the occupying forces were forced to supplement, improvise, and repair available facilities and to install many new facilities to meet their requirements.

The American Army and Navy established a world-wide network, using all previously known devices and developing many new ones. With the termination of the war the United States found itself in an outstanding position in the world of telecommunications, with a vast network of new military and naval installations supplementing the theretofore existing American-owned private commercial facilities. The disposition of this new network and the adaptation of it to world telecommunications, including American privately owned facilities became one of the prime duties of the telecommunications attaché abroad.

The continuing duties of telecommunications attachés are:

reporting on facilities and developments within the countries under their jurisdiction; formulating and recommending policies which may best promote American telecommunications interests; assisting American communications companies in their operations abroad; assisting in such negotiations as the United States Government may undertake with other governments on questions concerning telecommunications; and assisting private interests, both American and foreign, in obtaining and exchanging technical information on this subject.

In general United States policy on telecommunications, during the post-Nazi period, was directed toward the establishment of direct circuits, rapid communications, nondiscriminatory and low rates, and the standardization as far as possible, of telecommunications facilities.

In their efforts to fulfill the policies of the United States in the fields of telecommunications and of civil air aviation, both the telecommunications and the civil air attachés pioneered new territory and developed precedents for dealing with the kinds of economic problems which technology will make plentiful in the future.

The commercial reporting unit of the Paris Embassy was under the supervision of the Commercial Attaché. During the reconstruction period following World War II this position was filled by a Foreign Service officer who was formerly with the Department of Commerce, and who was transferred to the Department of State in the amalgamation of the two foreign services in 1939.

He was charged with the particular duty of supervising the preparation of the multifold and commercial reports for the Department of Commerce, and in the more general duty of promoting American trade with France, and protecting American trade interests. His unit prepared weekly, monthly, quarterly, and annual economic surveys; replied to inquiries from the Bureau of Foreign and Domestic Commerce on subjects ranging from abrasives to zippers; collected information on behalf of American firms and private individuals who saw in France a possible market, and for importers who desired to ascertain the availability of various articles; drafted much of the Embassy's correspondence with the Foreign Office and the Department of State on trade problems; and, not least in importance, gave counsel to American and French businessmen who called at the Embassy.

To cope with the extensive range of work allotted to it, the commercial unit was organized along the commodity pattern of the Bureau of Foreign and Domestic Commerce in Washington. There were twelve officers, including specialists in chemicals and drugs; lumber, paper and paper products; ceramics, wines, and specialties; motion pictures, motive products; machinery and electrical equipment; insurance and patents; and another who gave his entire time to the preparation of World Trade Directory Reports.

A part of the service which the Foreign Service and the Office of International Trade (formerly a service of the Bureau of Foreign and Domestic Commerce) render to the American business man is to maintain an up-to-date file of reports on all foreign firms and individuals of importance to American trade interests. These reports are prepared by Foreign Service officers, but made available by the Department of Commerce.

Owing to the war no reports of this character had reached the Department of Commerce from France for a period of four years. One of the first tasks of the Embassy upon its reopening was the overhauling of its file of old World Trade Directory reports. In 1945 no less than a thousand were prepared and forwarded through the Department of State to the Bureau of Foreign and Domestic Commerce. As these reports are subject to periodic revision, the work is a continuing process, not only in Paris but at every post where a mission or consulate exists throughout the world.

In the discharge of his task, the commercial attaché seeks to furnish the most specific and complete assistance possible to American Government agencies and American businessmen. His objectives are to supply information that can be quickly translated into effective operations by the government, or the interested firm or individual. Above all the commercial reporting unit must be constantly at work to keep Washington informed of every change in French laws and regulations which may affect commercial exchange between the two countries.

Some notion of the volume of work performed in the commercial reporting unit of the Embassy may be gained from the fact that—during 1945 and 1946—it prepared detailed, factual replies to more than five hundred letters each month. There were on the average, a dozen calls by businessmen each day.

If an American businessman visits France it is to the commercial unit of the Embassy that he should first direct his steps after his arrival. He will be given a clear, concise account of general conditions and a more detailed picture of the circumstances affecting his particular enterprise. He may be saved untold harassment and the shifting about from one bureau to another by taking advantage of this service rendered by the American Government.

An interesting and typical instance of this specialized assistance rendered by the Embassy occurred in 1945. An American manufacturer came in search of information concerning French developments in television. The Commercial Attaché and the Telecommunications Attaché together arranged a visit to the *Compagnie des Compteurs,* which produced television sets in some respects superior to those being manufactured in the United States. The American was given full details and a special demonstration of the sets and equipment. He was also put in touch with the Gaumont Company, one of the leading French producers of motion pictures.

Subsequently, the Embassy was able to reciprocate the courtesies extended by the French, by giving the president of the Gaumont Company, who was also director general of the *Compagnie des Compteurs,* letters of introduction to appropriate officials of the Bureau of Foreign and Domestic Commerce. Thus, the French businessman when he visited the United States to study American technological developments in the field of motion pictures and television, had the way smoothed for him.

The commercial section of the Embassy regularly supplies French enterprisers with exact information concerning the potential American market for his product—whether it be fashions or *foie gras*—and the conditions under which he may export it to the United States.

Agricultural attachés are assigned to missions in those countries where agricultural production is important to the United States. An agricultural and assistant agricultural attaché are normally assigned to the Paris Embassy. It is the practice for one of the two to be an agricultural economist.

In general, agricultural attachés, under the supervision of the chief of mission, undertake all those reporting activities on agriculture required by agencies of the United States Government. During the post-Nazi reconstruction, the schedule in France required the preparation of no less than seventy-four commodity reports each year. These ranged from dairy products, fruits, nuts, and tobacco to such outstanding French crops as wine, potatoes, and wheat. In addition, special reports were made when any new agricultural problems developed—which was often.

Both the importance and the nature of the agricultural attaché's work depend upon time and place. For example, the Agricultural Attaché is one of the most important members of the staff of the American Ambassador to Cuba. One reason is that the Cuban sugar crop furnishes a large part of the world supply and in consequence affects the American sugar market so powerfully that reporting on the condition of the crop and its estimated output is necessary in achieving economic balance in the United States.

Before the last war the work of agricultural attachés in France was concerned primarily with commodity reporting, having in view largely commercial trade movements. In the period immediately following the liberation the paramount problem of our agricultural attachés was estimating France's food requirements and planning how those needs might be met.

The food crisis throughout Europe made the position of the wheat crop both in France and French North Africa, particularly important. Accordingly, monthly reports were made from Paris on the wheat situation in those areas, in addition to reports on the over-all food outlook. During a period when France was passing through one of its most severe food crises, and obtaining a bare minimum of food for survival was the consuming problem of existence, the Agricultural Attaché and his assistant met weekly with officials of the French Ministry of Food and with Allied military representatives in an effort to work out means for supplying current needs in the face of such over-all problems as shipping, available food resources, and the comparative needs of other areas.

To make an adequate estimate of France's food requirements, the Agricultural Attachés found it necessary to study the French black and grey markets. It did not suffice to estimate France's needs on the basis of normal food distribution,

[1 3 7]

when a large part of the supply was moving through illegitimate channels, outside official supervision and hence outside the realm of official statistics.

Investigators of the Embassy found that urban consumers not only received food packages, but supplemented their supplies—so to speak—by hand. On Sunday when the Assistant Agricultural Attaché was traveling on the Paris *metro* he was startled by the quack of a goose in the basket borne by a chic Parisienne. His surprise was turned to amusement when the quack was answered by quacks from baskets borne by two other travelers in the subway, and by the cackle of a concealed hen. Inquiry disclosed that thousands of Parisians, finding the government rations insufficient for their needs, were going out on Sundays to the end of the *metro* line, tramping into the country, and purchasing illegally from producers. If these and other practices had not been taken into account, in the estimation of the amount of food finding its way to the consumer in France in 1944 and 1945, a wholly distorted view of France's needs, serious as they actually were, would have been conveyed to Washington. As a consequence, France might have been oversupplied, to the detriment of consumers in other countries where food needs were even more desperate.

By the patience brought to bear upon the problem and the assistance rendered the French authorities in meeting their nation's food needs, these attachés and our mission created immeasurable good will. This will help the mission to function effectively for a long time to come. It may make for better understanding between France and the United States. For, if the way to a man's heart is through his stomach, the same may be no less true of a nation, particularly one where food has traditionally played so great a part in the life of the individual as in France.

An important general function of the Agricultural Attaché

in France as elsewhere, is to bring to the people the forward-looking, scientific help which the county farm agent brings to rural communities in America. This attaché facilitates the introduction of improved seeds and disseminates information regarding improved agricultural methods. He reports all useful information concerning the technology of agriculture in the country of his residence. The improvement of agriculture in France, to which the Agricultural Attaché normally contributes, may have far-reaching results. Greater efficiency will raise the standard of living and with increased prosperity will come the greater purchasing power which will make France a better market for American goods.

The finance and statistics unit reports French statistics on such subjects as population and migration, national income, industrial production, domestic trade, internal price levels, wages and employment, and foreign trade—in short, all the data which may assist in evaluating the financial situation of the country. In addition, the finance and statistics unit reports on conditions, operations, and policies which may affect international finance. For example, the French balance of payments, the public debt, the budget, operations of the Bank of France, and the control of exchange. These reports are useful not only to the Department of State, but also to the planners and executives in the Department of Commerce, Treasury, Federal Reserve System, the Export-Import Bank—and a relatively small, but influential group of private citizens.

The postwar head of the unit performed duties equivalent to those of a financial attaché. In the early days of his career as a Foreign Service officer, he showed an aptitude for financial reporting. To fit him especially for his responsibilities—which were very heavy, since his reporting might influence such important decisions as the size of a United States loan to France

—he was assigned by the Department several years ago to take special courses of instruction in finance at the Littman School at Harvard University.

Finance and statistics are by no means so dull and unexciting as they sound. Money is a thread woven throughout the entire life of a people, and this unit of the Embassy sometimes found itself reporting on surprising affairs. For example, horse races.

As a means of reducing the currency in circulation below a dangerously inflated level, and ascertaining the whereabouts of funds, the French Government in 1945 changed the form of its notes. Holders of notes currently in circulation were given the period June 4-15, to make the exchange, after which the old notes became invalid. In addition to reducing the circulation by 150,000,000 francs in notes which were not presented for exchange owing to their loss or to the fear of the holders to declare them, the episode brought out of hiding some interesting and curious facts of French life after the occupation.

A fifteen-year-old schoolboy in Paris appeared at the exchange windows and presented no less than 50,000,000 francs for conversion into the new banknotes. Inquiry by the authorities disclosed that he had acquired this sum in black-market operations.

Not all holders, however, were as naïve as the schoolboy. When the change was first announced to a startled public, holders of large quantities of notes resorted to every conceivable device to avoid disclosing that they had them—and still not lose money. One of the most ingenious methods which came to the notice of the Embassy, was the placing on June 3 of huge wagers on a horse scheduled to run in a race on June 16. When the horse was scratched, by previous agreement between the layers of the wagers and the owner, the bettors obtained new notes to the amount of their bets without having to pass through government channels.

The financial attaché is also responsible for taking the necessary action to protect American interests in financial matters. For example, just after the war he was active in obtaining the release to American firms of dollars for merchandise sold in France before the war, for which payment had been made in francs. The release of dollars for the payment of accrued interest, dividends and royalties on patents and trade marks was also effected by the Embassy, the whole amounting to some $10,000,000.

Finance played so large a part in the transitional economic calculations of every country that the Embassy had to be constantly alert to protect American interests from discriminatory treatment in taxation, exchange control, and in other financial fields. In 1945 the French Government, with a view to financing reconstruction, imposed a "National Solidarity" tax, constituting a direct levy on capital and on enrichment gained during the war. This unusual and sweeping fiscal measure fell heavily on American citizens residing in France. For not only their holdings in France, but their assets in the United States as well were subject to taxation under it. The Embassy endeavored to obtain adjustment of the legislation insofar as it affected American citizens, on a wholly nondiscriminatory and equitable basis.

Developments during the war caused the State Department to assign certain missions, including the Embassy in Paris, a petroleum attaché responsible to the chief of mission through the counsellor for economic affairs. The first was appointed early in the war, to London.

` The petroleum attaché acts as technical advisor and principal reporting officer on all matters pertaining to the petroleum industry. In Paris, in addition to reporting on all

French legislation and trends affecting petroleum and, specifically, American petroleum interests, the Petroleum Attaché assisted in carrying out American official oil policy and in the protection and promotion of the legitimate interests of the American petroleum industry abroad. He was responsible not only for France but also for Belgium, Luxembourg, Switzerland, and all of French North Africa.

The establishment of a separate commercial policy unit in the economic section of the Paris Embassy was occasioned by:

1. A recognition of the need for commercial policy reporting as distinguished from the tradition trade promotion and trade protection activities of the commercial attaché. The basic reason for this division of labor was the increasing influence of economic policy, not only upon commerce, agriculture, and industry, but on politics as well. Conversely, politics influences economic policy; in reporting the two can seldom be entirely divorced.

2. The need for implementing proposed United States plans for postwar commercial policy. The objectives of these plans were agreements with France and other countries relating to tariff and other barriers to international trade, commodity agreements, cartel policy, and full employment.

The functions of the commercial policy unit in the Paris Embassy included a constant survey of the entire field of commercial policy, and reporting upon general trends in policy, actual or anticipated.

In reporting on commercial policy during the post-Nazi period, the responsible officer was guided by the vital interests of the United States in the reconstruction and expansion of world trade on a sound economic basis. To make possible that reconstruction and expansion, the United States Government considered the following measures essential:

1. The general relaxation of tariffs and other barriers to world trade.

2. The elimination, to the fullest extent practicable, of all forms of discriminatory trade treatment.

3. The conduct of international trade, to the greatest practicable extent, by private enterprise.

Those officers dealing with commercial policy were also expected to bear in mind during the transitional period immediately following the close of hostilities, the desire of the Department that wartime trade controls be reduced or eliminated as rapidly as possible, and that such controls be not used as instruments of commercial policy.

These officers also followed the trend of public opinion regarding commercial policy, noting particularly those developments likely to indicate or influence the attitude of the French Government toward postwar international cooperation.

In addition to these general objectives the officers were expected to relate their reporting to the particular problems which were peculiar to the French situation.

After the liberation, French authorities were concerned less with the formulation of clearly defined commercial policies than with meeting *ad hoc* the multitudinous problems which plagued the restoration of the commerce of France. Improvisations were the order of the day.

These factors made the task of the commercial policy unit of the Embassy all the more difficult. They also made it critically important to keep the Department of State and other interested governmental agencies as fully informed as possible. The more difficult the situation of a nation, and the more fluid its policy, the more vital prompt and expert reporting by Foreign Service officers becomes to the decision makers in our own government.

XII

THE EMBASSY'S INFORMATION
AND
CULTURAL RELATIONS SECTION

THE OFFICERS who first staffed this section—which was created shortly after the close of World War II—were pioneers in a new area of diplomacy. During the past half century the old confines, established when governments dealt entirely with governments, have broken down on all sides—as previous passages on the other sections of the Embassy have made clear. The establishment of the information and cultural relations section of the Paris Embassy was the logical development of this trend. In today's world it is necessary for the *peoples* of all countries to understand one another, learn from one another, and work together on mutual problems. Diplomatic missions must be transfer points between them. The information and cultural relations section of the Embassy broadens the contact between Frenchmen and Americans into new areas.

Since it was pioneering, the activities of this section during the postwar period may be only a curtain raiser and not a representative sample of the work as it will be when experience and precedent have established the most effective patterns of organization and operation. However, the work of pioneers is as important and as interesting as that of men who come after them and develop the territory they explore. Moreover, it is quite certain that future diplomacy in the area of information and cultural relations will have the same basic goals which underlie present activities. And it is certain that these activities will continue—if for no other reason than that other nations are pursuing them with great vigor and skill. The United States has, in fact, lagged far behind in this arm of diplomacy. British lecturers and other information providers are credited with winning American support to the Allied cause during World War I. The U.S.S.R. has established in many countries organizations such as France-U.S.S.R. to disseminate favorable information concerning the Soviet and to interpret its culture and policies. It might have been possible to forestall the insidious work of the Nazis and Fascists in countries which they readied for the fall, had we been prepared to disseminate truth as vigorously as their industrious termites spread falsehood and slander.

The main objectives of the information and cultural relations section were to support the aims of American policy and to advance Franco-American relations. The staff accomplished these objectives by bringing to the French people a true, well-rounded picture of American life; by correcting false impressions of America, and guarding against attitudes antagonistic to American policies and actions; and by facilitating exchange of the techniques and knowledge of contemporary civilization.

In 1945 the State Department announced the following program for world wide activities in the field of information and cultural relations:

1. Exchange of students, of scholars and of technicians and other experts with special knowledge and skills, with the Department of State acting as the co-ordinating agency for twenty-six government departments and bureaus having information programs.

2. Maintenance and servicing of American libraries of information in sixty countries abroad.

3. Dissemination of a daily wireless bulletin to American diplomatic missions throughout the world containing the full texts, or textual excerpts of important official pronouncements.

4. Forwarding to missions abroad, by mail, documentary material relating to the United States, including still photographs.

5. Preparation of photo-exhibits and films for showing in foreign countries.

6. Continuation of the bimonthly illustrated magazines in Russian for distribution in the Soviet Union, where privately published magazines are barred.

7. Acquiring, adapting, and scoring in foreign languages of newsreels and documentary films concerning the United States.

8. Operation under the Department of State of short-wave broadcasting in eighteen foreign languages.*

This program was put into the hands of a staff made up of officers who had been carrying on the State Department's own cultural affairs program, assumed in 1938, and some employees of two separate, wartime organizations—the Office of Inter-American Affairs, and the Office of War Information—whose functions were absorbed by the State Department in 1946.

In Paris, the information and cultural relations section was placed under the direction of a single officer, but divided into three subsections; press, information, and cultural relations.

The press attaché's function in an embassy is analogous to that of the director of public relations in a government bureau or large business. In all press matters he is the official link between the embassy, and foreign officialdom, American and

* In 1947 this had increased to twenty-five languages.

foreign newspapermen, and similar professional contacts. Releases to the press are prepared and issued either on the initiative of the press attaché, with the concurrence of the ambassador, or on the initiative of the ambassador himself or one of his principal advisers. It is a recognized duty on the part of the press attaché to make the chief of mission widely known as the representative of the United States, and create the most favorable possible place for him in public esteem. This is accomplished by arranging for the ambassador's appearance before the microphone and in newsreels and in obtaining favorable publicity for him in the press. It is a difficult assignment, because experienced chiefs are well aware that those in high places are wary of confiding in diplomats who talk a great deal to the press. The press attaché must, therefore, be very circumspect and make certain that he promotes only publicity which is in the national interest, avoiding that which merely serves personal aggrandizement.

There are many other general duties of a press attaché. He gives practical advice and assistance to American newspapermen; arranges press conferences for important American officials passing through the country of his assignment; prepares a daily résumé for the State Department on editorial opinion and a weekly review of periodicals, keeping Washington informed of all matters of interest to the French press.

A striking example of how an alert press attaché may use the prestige of the Ambassador's position to promote good will for the United States is the story behind "What the War Really Did to France"—an article which appeared in the *American Magazine* for April, 1945 under the signature of Ambassador Caffery.

The office of the Press Attaché detected, soon after the reopening of the Paris Embassy, that the principal grievance of the French people against the United States was the belief that the American people did not understand what France had suffered from the war. It was a time when the press was making much of the cynical observation of an American businessman that the presence of brass doorknobs on the Ritz Hotel clearly evidenced that Paris had been untouched by the German occupation, and that all was for the best in France in this best of all possible worlds.

The problem was debated in the Embassy and many minds were brought to bear upon it. The Press Attaché took a sheet of paper and on it he wrote: "Let us find the answer to the French complaints." The ensuing analysis brought forth a statement of the problem which was used as the opening paragraph of the article eventually published by the Ambassador. It read:

"There has been an impression in the United States and even among Americans in the European theater that France suffered comparatively little material and moral damage as a result of her war and four years of German occupation."

The article proceeded to develop the proof to the contrary, with many tragic examples; it also showed how Americans could have gained a totally false impression.

It was not enough, however, to get the article published in the United States. The essential thing was to let the French people know that the Ambassador was alive to their situation and was doing his utmost to acquaint American people with the facts. Arrangements were made for republication of the article in a leading French weekly and circulation of thousands of reprints.

The response was immediate and overwhelming. The French press welcomed the article as an unmistakable testimonial of both American sympathy and deep understanding. One editorial writer went so far as to say that the brilliant analysis of the Ambassador went farther in revealing the reality than any Frenchman could have done. More than a thousand Frenchmen were inspired to write personally to the Ambassador to express their deeply felt appreciation. To these and thousands of other readers, the article showed beyond dispute that, in this most distressful hour, the United States and its Ambassador understood and appreciated the sorely tried heart of France, however disconsolate its beating.

As a furnisher-of-news, the press attaché will always have a certain amount of difficulty with the secretive policies and indifference which often lead government agencies and officials to disregard the legitimate demands of a news-hungry world. A notable example of the discomfiture suffered by the Press Attaché and unnecessary exacerbation of local American correspondents, is afforded in the official veil of secrecy imposed upon the journey through Paris of Secretary of State Byrnes, upon his visit to Moscow in late 1945.

As the French had not been invited to this Conference of Foreign Ministers of the Big Three, orders were given by Washington that the Embassy was to keep Secretary Byrnes' stopover secret from both American and French newspapermen. The Paris correspondents knew that Mr. Byrnes was leaving Washington for Moscow, and it needed no great stretch of the imagination for them to conclude, when the American Ambassador drove out of Paris to the Orly airfield, that he was meeting some very distinguished American official. Who could it be but Mr. Byrnes? The Embassy, however, had been instructed to say nothing and, in answer to hundreds of telephone calls from irate correspondents, the Embassy had "nothing to say." The Press Attaché would have preferred to take the press, at least the American section, into the Embassy's confidence and to have disclosed the truth with a request that nothing be published locally until after the Secretary had left. But the word had gone out that the Embassy must be mute—and an infuriating muteness it was to correspondents who, no doubt, interpreted the incident as one more example of the stupidity of Foreign Service officers.

The information subsection was, by reason of its multifarious duties, divided into a number of units; press, radio, film, speaker's bureau, regional offices, and documentation center.

The press unit was distinct from the office of the Press Attaché because it dealt in basic, background information rather than public relations and "spot" news. It issued five days a week a publication known as *U.S.A.* based on the Department's radio bulletin, and containing material not available through commercial press agencies. *U.S.A.* was distributed to every newspaper in France, to leading officials, libraries, schools, and universities. The mailing list for Paris alone totalled nine hundred. As not all French newspapers were financially able or sufficiently interested to subscribe to American news agencies' services, it is obvious that without this service rendered by the United States Government through its information service little of constructive American news would have found its way into the French press as a whole. During the last quarter of 1945 no less than seventy items from *U.S.A.* were reproduced monthly in the important French language press of Paris alone; use of the material by the provincial press was comparable.

Another publication of the information unit was *Le Document de la Semaine,* a weekly bulletin, printed in six thousand copies and distributed to newspapers, magazines, leading officials, libraries, and educational institutions. The material was drawn from articles supplied from Washington and covered such topics as "American Views on the Economic Reconstruction of Europe," "Political Parties in the United States," "The American Constitution," and "How America Votes."

Special features, based on material received from the Department of State were supplied at the specific request of newspapers and periodicals. Three hundred and fourteen feature articles, dealing with various aspects of American life, were published in the Paris press during the last three months of 1945. Material supplied by the Embassy's information section found its way into such publications as the *Techniques Architectures* (for November, 1945), a model of the printing art on which the French rightfully pride themselves.

A further publication of the information unit was the *Bulletin Economique,* issued weekly. This dealt with American economic and financial developments, and it was distributed to the fifteen leading French financial newspapers and reviews, and to a few French officials.

In addition, the information unit made available both to the press and—in the form of exhibits to the public—still-life photographs drawn from a library of 30,000 prints. It also maintained a picture file for the special use of journalists and, by personal liaison with the press, endeavored to create a favorable atmosphere for the United States.

The radio subsection of the information unit arranged interviews with prominent Americans and provided both special musical events by guest performers and recordings to the French networks. This service was rendered regularly in the Embassy's continuing attempt to promote good will. As occasion arose, special programs were arranged to remove misconceptions and revise public attitudes unfavorable to the interests of the United States.

The film unit of the Embassy was concerned with promoting a better appreciation of the United States through the medium of the screen. Noncommercial films depicting various facets of American life, whose distribution through normal commercial channels was not feasible for monetary reasons, were made available to various French groups, such as schools, agricultural co-operatives, Franco-American clubs, village halls, and religious circles. In the last quarter of 1945 fifty-two such films were shown to audiences of more than a million people.

A form of international contact which was used to great advantage by other nations long before it was employed by the United States is the lecture platform.

Belatedly we have begun to use public speakers systematically to advance American interests among the people of other nations. In Paris the Embassy's speaker's bureau organized lecture tours throughout France, sending such personages as were available; ranking Foreign Service officers and Army officers, and distinguished American residents and visitors.

The French nation affords a very appreciative and wide audience to the American public speaker who has an adequate command of the language and the capacity to present a subject attractively. During the postwar period the supply of lecturers possessing these qualifications was limited. To serve American interests effectively on French platforms requires a steady flow of speakers from universities, professional associations, industrial and trade associations, learned societies, trade unions, and brotherhoods. Nor can any speaker who is either intellectually or socially a snob serve his country effectively.

A new world is rising in France far removed from the salons of the Faubourg St. Germain. It is a world of the working man who has no speaking acquaintance with English, and for whom the traditional lecturer, more used to pleasing a fashionable public than facing realities, has little appeal. The information service of the Paris Embassy was fully alive to this problem, sought to draw more and more speakers from organized labor and from among socially conscious Americans.

To ensure adequate information work to meet the restricted but no less real needs of the provinces, the information and cultural relations section established regional outposts at Marseilles, Lyons, and Toulouse, and projected others. These outposts performed in miniature the same functions in their respective districts as the information section of the Embassy.

Probably no single activity of the information section in Paris has come more directly in contact with the public or has done more to make the United States known than the documentation center. Here at the Place de l'Opéra, the heart of Paris, a reference library and reading room was maintained during 1945 and 1946. It was visited on the average by five hundred French men and women daily. Here French doctors came to consult files of American medical publications from which they had been cut off by six years of war and physical and cultural isolation. Scientists, teachers, and students throng the rooms in their avid thirst for information.

"Cultural relations" is superficially a vague and idealistic term. On closer examination it becomes as concrete and practical a matter as economics. For "culture" means a people's way of living. It embraces those activities which, taken all together, differentiate the people who live in one country or region from those who live elsewhere.

The work of the cultural relations subsection of the Paris Embassy was instituted on January 30, 1945. At first it was almost pure pioneering. The immediate task of the officer-in-charge was to stimulate interest in American achievements in the fields of education, literature, fine arts, music, the theatrical arts, and documentary films; to encourage intellectual leaders to visit the United States, and to report to the Department on cultural trends in France.

[153]

As the existence of the Cultural Relations Attaché was unknown to the public, he had to take the initiative in making such personal contacts as might best promote his assigned objectives. To that end he called on the publisher of an illustrated book which he had admired, the director of the Cinématique Française whose lectures on documentary films he had seen announced; he attended the lectures of eminent university professors in order to be able to speak to them at the conclusion, to make their acquaintance, and to let them know of the interest of the Embassy in cultural relations between the United States and France. Contacts were also established with the French Director General of Cultural Relations, and interested officials in the French Ministries of Education and Information.

During his first year the Cultural Relations Attaché succeeded in gaining a thorough understanding of current French cultural trends, made himself familiar with all important educational, scientific, and cultural organizations in France, and established friendly and continuing contacts with most of these. The Embassy, therefore, achieved a most satisfactory position from which to assist American intellectuals to establish working contacts with their French colleagues and, reciprocally, to furnish information to French organizations on their fields of interest in the United States. The cultural relations subsection assisted in arranging for the visit to the United States of a number of French students, teachers, lecturers, and intellectuals sponsored by the French Government.

By the middle of 1946, this work was so far advanced that the Embassy could plan formation of a Franco-American Cultural Center to comprise an Institute of American Studies, the American Library in Paris, and a Franco-American Cultural Institute; the exchange of students between the two countries on a progressively larger scale; increasing exchange of professors and cultural leaders; and means for facilitating a greater exchange of scientific, educational, and general cultural material between France and the United States. These plans were not confined to cultural exchange in its narrow and somewhat aristocratic sense. The objective was to increase knowledge of American culture in all its diverse forms.

APPENDIX A

THE FOREIGN SERVICE ACT

[Public Law 724—79th Congress]
[Chapter 957—2d Session]
[H. R. 6967]

AN ACT

To improve, strengthen, and expand the Foreign Service of the United States and to consolidate and revise the laws relating to its administration.

Be it enacted by the Senate and House of Representatives of the United States of America in Congress assembled,

TITLE I—SHORT TITLE, OBJECTIVES, AND DEFINITIONS

Part A—Short Title

Sec. 101. Titles I to X, inclusive, of this Act may be cited as the "Foreign Service Act of 1946".

Part B—Objectives

Sec. 111. The Congress hereby declares that the objectives of this Act are to develop and strengthen the Foreign Service of the United States so as—

(1) to enable the Foreign Service effectively to serve abroad the interests of the United States;

(2) to insure that the officers and employees of the Foreign Service are broadly representative of the American people and are aware of and fully informed in respect to current trends in American life;

(3) to enable the Foreign Service adequately to fulfill the functions devolving on it by reason of the transfer to the Department of State of functions heretofore performed by other Government agencies;

(4) to provide improvements in the recruitment and training of the personnel of the Foreign Service;

(5) to provide that promotions leading to positions of authority and responsibility shall be on the basis of merit and to insure the selection on an impartial basis of outstanding persons for such positions;

(6) to provide for the temporary appointment or assignment to the Foreign Service of representative and outstanding citizens of the United States possessing special skills and abilities;

(7) to provide salaries, allowances, and benefits that will permit the Foreign Service to draw its personnel from all walks of American life and to appoint persons to the highest positions in the Service solely on the basis of their demonstrated ability;

(8) to provide a flexible and comprehensive framework for the direction of the Foreign Service in accordance with modern practices in public administration; and

(9) to codify into one Act all provisions of law relating to the administration of the Foreign Service.

PART C—DEFINITIONS

SEC. 121. When used in this Act, the term—

(1) "Service" means the Foreign Service of the United States;

(2) "Secretary" means the Secretary of State;

(3) "Department" means the Department of State;

(4) "Government agency" means any executive department, board, bureau, commission, or other agency in the executive branch of the Federal Government, or any corporation wholly

owned (either directly or through one or more corporations) by the United States;

(5) "Government" means the Government of the United States of America;

(6) "Continental United States" means the States and the District of Columbia;

(7) "Abroad" means all areas not included in the continental United States as defined in paragraph (6) of this section;

(8) "Principal officer" means the officer in charge of an embassy, legation, or other diplomatic mission or of a consulate general, consulate, or vice consulate of the United States; and

(9) "Chief of mission" means a principal officer appointed by the President, by and with the advice and consent of the Senate, to be in charge of an embassy or legation or other diplomatic mission of the United States, or any person assigned under the terms of this Act to be minister resident, chargé d'affaires, commissioner, or diplomatic agent.

TITLE II—GOVERNING BODIES FOR THE DIRECTION OF THE SERVICE

Part A—Officers

DIRECTOR GENERAL

SEC. 201. The Service shall be administered by a Director General of the Foreign Service, hereinafter referred to as the Director General, who shall be appointed by the Secretary from among Foreign Service officers in the class of career minister or in class 1. Under the general supervision of the Secretary and the Assistant Secretary of State in charge of the administration of the Department, the Director General shall, in addition to administering the Service and performing the duties specifically vested in him by this or any other Act, coordinate the activities of the Service with the needs of the Department and of other Government agencies and direct the performance by officers and employees of the Service of the duties imposed on them by the terms of any law or by any order or regulation issued pursuant to law or by any international agreement to which the United States is a party.

DEPUTY DIRECTOR GENERAL

SEC. 202. The Director General shall be assisted by a Deputy Director General of the Foreign Service, hereinafter referred to as the Deputy Director General, who shall be appointed by the Secretary. If he is a Foreign Service officer, he shall be selected from among officers in the class of career minister or in class 1. The Deputy Director General shall act in the place of the Director General in the event of his absence or incapacity.

PART B—BOARDS

BOARD OF THE FOREIGN SERVICE

SEC. 211. (a) The Board of the Foreign Service shall be composed of the Assistant Secretary of State in charge of the administration of the Department, who shall be Chairman; two other Assistant Secretaries of State, designated by the Secretary to serve on the Board; the Director General; and one representative each, occupying positions with comparable responsibilities, from the Departments of Agriculture, Commerce, and Labor, designated, respectively, by the heads of such departments. The Secretary may request the head of any other Government department to designate a representative, occupying a position with comparable responsibilities, to attend meetings of the Board whenever matters affecting the interest of such department are under consideration.

(b) The Board of the Foreign Service shall make recommendations to the Secretary concerning the functions of the Service; the policies and procedures to govern the selection, assignment, rating, and promotion of Foreign Service officers; and the policies and procedures to govern the administration and personnel management of the Service; and shall perform such other duties as are vested in it by other sections of this Act or by the terms of any other Act.

THE BOARD OF EXAMINERS FOR THE FOREIGN SERVICE

SEC. 212. (a) The Board of Examiners for the Foreign Service, shall, in accordance with regulations prescribed by the Secretary and under the general supervision of the Board of the Foreign Service, provide for and supervise the conduct of such examinations as may be given to candidates for appointment as Foreign Service officers in accordance with the provisions of sections 516 and 517 or to any other person to whom an examination for admission to the Service shall be given in accordance with the provisions of this or any other Act or any regulations issued pursuant thereto, and provide for such procedures as may be necessary to determine the loyalty of such persons to the United States and their attachment to the principles of the Constitution.

(b) The membership of the Board of Examiners for the Foreign Service, not more than half of which shall consist of Foreign Service officers, shall be constituted in accordance with regulations prescribed by the Secretary.

TITLE III—DUTIES

PART A—GENERAL DUTIES

COMPLIANCE WITH TERMS OF STATUTES, INTERNATIONAL AGREEMENTS, AND EXECUTIVE ORDERS

SEC. 301. Officers and employees of the Service shall, under the direction of the Secretary, represent abroad the interests of the United States and shall perform the duties and comply with the obligations resulting from the nature of their appointments or assignments or imposed on them by the terms of any law or by any order or regulation issued pursuant to law or by any international agreement to which the United States is a party.

DUTIES FOR WHICH REGULATIONS MAY BE PRESCRIBED

SEC. 302. The Secretary shall, except in an instance where the authority is specifically vested in the President, have authority to prescribe regulations not inconsistent with the Constitution and the laws of the United States in relation to the duties, functions, and obligations of officers and employees of the Service and the administration of the Service.

DELEGATION OF AUTHORITY TO PRESCRIBE REGULATIONS

SEC. 303. In cases where authority to prescribe regulations relating to the Service or the duties and obligations of officers and employees of the Service is specifically vested in the President by the terms of this or any other Act, the President may, nevertheless, authorize the Secretary to prescribe such regulations.

Part B—Services for Government Agencies and Other Establishments of the Government

SEC. 311. The officers and employees of the Service shall, under such regulations as the President may prescribe, perform duties and functions in behalf of any Government agency or any other establishment of the Government requiring their services, including those in the legislative and judicial branches, but the absence of such regulations shall not preclude officers and employees of the Service from acting for and on behalf of any such Government agency or establishment whenever it shall, through the Department, request their services.

TITLE IV—CATEGORIES AND SALARIES OF PERSONNEL

Part A—Categories of Personnel

SEC. 401. The personnel of the Service shall consist of the following categories of officers and employees:

(1) Chiefs of mission, who shall be appointed or assigned in accordance with the provisions of section 501;

(2) Foreign Service officers, who shall be appointed in accordance with section 511, including those serving as chiefs of mission;

(3) Foreign Service Reserve officers, who shall be assigned to the Service on a temporary basis from Government agencies or appointed on a temporary basis from outside the Government in accordance with the provisions of section 522, in order to make available to the Service such specialized skills as may from time to time be required;

(4) Foreign Service staff officers and employees, who shall be appointed in accordance with the provisions of section 531 and who shall include all personnel who are citizens of the United States, not comprehended under paragraphs (1), (2), (3), and (6) of this section, and who shall occupy positions with technical, administrative, fiscal, clerical, or custodial responsibilities.

[162]

(5) Alien clerks and employees, who shall be appointed in accordance with the provisions of section 541; and

(6) Consular agents, who shall be appointed in accordance with the provisions of section 551.

PART B—SALARIES

CHIEFS OF MISSION

SEC. 411. The President shall for salary purposes classify into four classes the positions which are to be occupied by chiefs of mission. The per annum salaries of chiefs of mission within each class shall be as follows: Class 1, $25,000 per annum; class 2, $20,000; class 3, $17,500; and class 4, $15,000.

FOREIGN SERVICE OFFICERS

SEC. 412. There shall be seven classes of Foreign Service officers, including the class of career minister. The per annum salary of a career minister shall be $13,500. The per annum salaries of Foreign Service officers within each of the other classes shall be as follows:

Class 1, $12,000, $12,400, $12,800, $13,200, $13,500;

Class 2, $10,000, $10,350, $10,700, $11,050, $11,400, $11,750, $11,900;

Class 3, $8,000, $8,300, $8,600, $8,900, $9,200, $9,500, $9,800, $9,900;

Class 4, $6,000, $6,300, $6,600, $6,900, $7,200, $7,500, $7,800, $7,900;

Class 5, $4,500, $4,700, $4,900, $5,100, $5,300, $5,500, $5,700, $5,900;

Class 6, $3,300, $3,500, $3,700, $3,900, $4,100, $4,300, $4,400.

SALARIES AT WHICH FOREIGN SERVICE OFFICERS MAY BE APPOINTED

SEC. 413. (a) A person appointed as a Foreign Service officer of class 6 shall receive salary at that one of the rates provided for that class by section 412 which the Secretary shall, taking into consideration his age, qualifications, and experience, determine to be appropriate for him to receive.

(b) A person appointed as a Foreign Service officer of classes 1 through 5, inclusive, shall receive salary at the minimum rate provided for the class to which he has been appointed.

FOREIGN SERVICE RESERVE OFFICERS

SEC. 414. (a) There shall be six classes of Foreign Service Reserve officers, referred to hereafter as Reserve officers, which classes shall correspond to classes 1 to 6 of Foreign Service officers

(b) A Reserve officer shall receive salary at any one of the rate provided for the class to which he is appointed or assigned in accordance with the provisions of section 523.

(c) A person assigned as a Reserve officer from any Government agency shall receive his salary from appropriations provided for the Department during the period of his service as a Reserve officer.

FOREIGN SERVICE STAFF OFFICERS AND EMPLOYEES

SEC. 415. There shall be twenty-two classes of Foreign Service staff officers and employees, referred to hereafter as staff officers and employees. The per annum rates of salary of staff officers and employees within each class shall be as follows:

Class 1, $8,820, $9,120, $9,420, $9,720, $10,000;

Class 2, $8,100, $8,340, $8,580, $8,820, $9,120;

Class 3, $7,380, $7,620, $7,860, $8,100, $8,340;

Class 4, $6,660, $6,900, $7,140, $7,380, $7,620;

Class 5, $6,120, $6,300, $6,480, $6,660, $6,900, $7,140;

Class 6, $5,580, $5,760, $5,940, $6,120, $6,300, $6,480;

Class 7, $5,040, $5,220, $5,400, $5,580, $5,760, $5,940;

Class 8, $4,500, $4,680, $4,860, $5,040, $5,220, $5,400;

Class 9, $3,960, $4,140, $4,320, $4,500, $4,680, $4,860;

Class 10, $3,600, $3,720, $3,840, $3,960, $4,140, $4,320, $4,500;

Class 11, $3,240, $3,360, $3,480, $3,600, $3,720, $3,840, $3,960;

Class 12, $2,880, $3,000, $3,120, $3,240, $3,360, $3,480, $3,600;

Class 13, $2,520, $2,640, $2,760, $2,880, $3,000, $3,120, $3,240;

Class 14, $2,160, $2,280, $2,400, $2,520, $2,640, $2,760, $2,880;

Class 15, $1,980, $2,040, $2,100, $2,160, $2,280, $2,400, $2,520;

Class 16, $1,800, $1,860, $1,920, $1,980, $2,040, $2,100, $2,160;

Class 17, $1,620, $1,680, $1,740, $1,800, $1,860, $1,920, $1,980;

Class 18, $1,440, $1,500, $1,560, $1,620, $1,680, $1,740, $1,800;

Class 19, $1,260, $1,320, $1,380, $1,440, $1,500, $1,560, $1,620;

Class 20, $1,080, $1,140, $1,200, $1,260, $1,320, $1,380, $1,440;

Class 21, $900, $960, $1,020, $1,080, $1,140, $1,200, $1,260;

Class 22, $720, $780, $840, $900, $960, $1,020, $1,080.

SALARIES AT WHICH FOREIGN SERVICE STAFF OFFICERS AND EMPLOYEES MAY BE APPOINTED

SEC. 416. A person appointed as a staff officer or employee shall receive salary at the minimum rate provided for the class to which appointed except as otherwise provided in accordance with the provisions of Part E of this title.

SALARIES OF ALIEN CLERKS AND EMPLOYEES

SEC. 417. The salary or compensation of an alien clerk or employee shall be fixed by the Secretary in accordance with such regulations as he shall prescribe and, as soon as practicable, in accordance with the provisions of section 444 (b). The salary or compensation of an alien clerk or employee fixed on a per annum basis may, notwithstanding the provisions of any other law, be payable on a weekly or biweekly basis. When a one- or two-week pay period of such a clerk or employee begins in one fiscal year and ends in another, the gross amount of the earnings for such pay period may be regarded as a charge against the appropriation or allotment current at the end of such pay period.

SALARIES OF CONSULAR AGENTS

SEC. 418. The salary or compensation of a consular agent shall be fixed by the Secretary in accordance with such regulations as he shall prescribe and, as soon as practicable, in accordance with the provisions of section 445.

PART C—SALARIES OF OFFICERS TEMPORARILY IN CHARGE

AS CHARGÉS D'AFFAIRES AD INTERIM

SEC. 421. For such time as any Foreign Service officer shall be authorized to act as chargé d'affaires ad interim at the post to which he is assigned, he shall receive, in addition to his basic salary as Foreign Service officer, compensation equal to that portion of the difference between such salary and the basic salary provided for the chief of mission as the Secretary may determine to be appropriate.

AS OFFICERS IN CHARGE OF CONSULATES GENERAL OR CONSULATES

SEC. 422. For such time as any Foreign Service officer or any consul or vice consul who is not a Foreign Service officer is temporarily in charge of a consulate general or consulate during the absence or incapacity of the principal officer, he shall receive, in addition to his basic salary as Foreign Service officer or consul or vice consul, compensation equal to that portion which the Secretary shall determine to be appropriate of the difference between such salary and the basic salary provided for the principal officer, or, if there be none, of the former principal officer.

PART D—TIME OF RECEIVING SALARY

CHIEFS OF MISSION

SEC. 431. (a) Under such regulations as the Secretary may prescribe, a chief of mission may be entitled to receive salary from the effective date of his appointment to the date marking his return to his place of residence at the conclusion of the period of his official service as chief of mission or the termination of time spent on authorized leave, whichever shall be later, but no chief of mission shall be entitled to receive salary while absent from his post whenever the Secretary shall find that such absence was without authorization or justification. If a chief of mission in one position is appointed as chief of mission in another position, he shall be entitled to receive the salary pertaining to the new position commencing on the effective date of the new appointment.

(b) The official services of a chief of mission shall not be deemed terminated by the appointment of a successor but shall continue until he has relinquished charge of the mission and has rendered such additional services to the Department as the Secretary may require him to render in the interests of the Government for a period not in excess of thirty days, exclusive of time spent in transit.

(c) During the service of a Foreign Service officer as chief of mission he shall receive, in addition to his salary as Foreign Service officer, compensation equal to the difference, if any, between such salary and the salary of the position to which he is appointed or assigned.

OTHER OFFICERS AND EMPLOYEES

SEC. 432. (a) Under such regulations as the Secretary may prescribe, any officer or employee appointed to the Service may be entitled to receive salary from the effective date of his appointment

[166]

to the date when he shall have returned to his place of residence at the conclusion of the period of his official service, or the termination of time spent on authorized leave, whichever shall be later, but no such officer or employee shall be entitled to receive salary while absent from his post whenever the Secretary shall find that such absence was without authorization or justification.

(b) A Foreign Service officer, appointed during a recess of the Senate, shall be paid salary from the effective date of his appointment until the end of the next session of the Senate, if he has not theretofore been confirmed by the Senate, or until his rejection by the Senate before the end of its next session.

(c) A Foreign Service officer promoted to a higher class shall receive salary at the rate prescribed in section 412 for the class to which he is promoted from the effective date of his appointment to such class. A Foreign Service officer promoted to a higher class during a recess of the Senate shall receive salary at the rate prescribed for the class to which he is promoted from the effective date of his appointment to such class until the end of the next session. If the Senate should reject or fail to confirm the promotion of such an officer during the session following the date of his promotion, the Foreign Service officer shall, unless he has become liable to separation in accordance with the provisions of section 633 or 634, be automatically reinstated in the class from which he was promoted and receive the salary he was receiving prior to his promotion, such reinstatement to be effective, in the event of rejection of the nomination, from the date of rejection; and in the event of the failure of the Senate to act on the nomination during the session following a promotion, from the termination of that session.

Part E—Classification

CLASSIFICATION OF POSITIONS IN THE FOREIGN SERVICE

Sec. 441. Under such regulations as he may prescribe, the Secretary shall classify all positions in the Service, including those positions at foreign posts which may be held by career ministers, and shall allocate all positions occupied or to be occupied by staff officers or employees to classes and subclasses established by sections 415 and 442, respectively, and by alien employees and consular agents to such classes as may be established by regulation.

ADMINISTRATIVE ESTABLISHMENT OF NEW GROUPS OF POSITIONS FOR FOREIGN SERVICE STAFF OFFICERS AND EMPLOYEES

SEC. 442. The Secretary may, whenever he deems such action to be in the interests of good administration and warranted by the nature of the duties and responsibilities of any group of positions occupied or to be occupied by staff officers and employees in comparison with other positions in the same class, establish by regulation for any such group of positions a minimum salary computed at any one of the rates of salary above the minimum for a given class but not in excess of the middle rate provided for that class in section 415. Such groups of positions shall, for the purposes of this Act, be known as subclasses.

ADMINISTRATIVE ESTABLISHMENT OF SALARY DIFFERENTIALS

SEC. 443. Whenever the President shall find and declare that the rates of salary provided for Foreign Service staff officers and employees in section 415 are inadequate for any positions allocated to any particular class or subclass, he may, under such regulations as he may prescribe, establish necessary schedules of differentials in the rates of salary prescribed for such classes or subclasses, but the differential in salary of a person holding any such position shall not exceed 25 per centum of the salary he would otherwise receive. Such differentials shall be granted only with respect to positions at posts at which extraordinarily difficult living conditions or excessive physical hardship prevail or at which notably unhealthful conditions exist. The Secretary shall prepare and maintain a list of such posts.

CLASSIFICATION OF POSITIONS OF ALIEN CLERKS AND EMPLOYEES

SEC. 444. (a) Upon the basis of the classification provided for in section 441, the Secretary shall, with the advice of the Board of the Foreign Service, from time to time prepare schedules of salaries for classes of positions of alien clerks and employees of the Service, which classes shall be established by regulation, and shall allocate all such positions to the appropriate classes.

(b) All alien employees in an area of comparatively uniform wage scales and standards of living, occupying positions of equal responsibility, shall receive equal pay except as there may be increases provided for length of service in accordance with uniform procedures.

SEC. 445. Upon the basis of the classification provided for in section 441, the Secretary shall, with the advice of the Board of the Foreign Service, from time to time prepare schedules of salaries for classes of positions of consular agents, which classes shall be established by regulation, and shall allocate all such positions to the appropriate classes.

EXEMPTION FROM THE APPLICATION OF THE CLASSIFICATION ACT

SEC. 446. Title II of the Act of November 26, 1940, entitled "An Act extending the classified executive Civil Service of the United States" (54 Stat. 1212; 5 U. S. C. 681), is hereby further amended by deleting paragraph (vii) of section 3 (d) and by substituting in lieu of the present language of paragraph (vi) of section 3 (d) the following language: "Offices or positions of officers and employees of the Foreign Service".

TITLE V—APPOINTMENTS AND ASSIGNMENTS

PART A—PRINCIPAL DIPLOMATIC REPRESENTATIVES

APPOINTMENTS

SEC. 501. (a) The President shall, by and with the advice and consent of the Senate, appoint ambassadors and ministers, including career ministers.

(b) The President may, in his discretion, assign any Foreign Service officer to serve as minister resident, chargé d'affaires, commissioner, or diplomatic agent for such period as the public interest may require.

LISTS OF FOREIGN SERVICE OFFICERS QUALIFIED TO BE CAREER MINISTERS OR CHIEFS OF MISSION TO BE FURNISHED TO THE PRESIDENT

SEC. 502. (a) The Secretary shall, on the basis of recommendations made by the Board of the Foreign Service, from time to time furnish the President with the names of Foreign Service officers qualified for appointment to the class of career minister together with pertinent information about such officers, but no person shall be appointed into the class of career minister who has not been appointed to serve as a chief of mission or appointed or assigned to serve in a position which, in the opinion of the Secretary, is of comparable importance. A list of such positions shall from time to time be published by the Secretary.

(b) The Secretary shall also, on the basis of recommendations made by the Board of the Foreign Service, from time to time furnish the President with the names of Foreign Service officers qualified for appointment or assignment as chief of mission, together with pertinent information about such officers, in order to assist the President in selecting qualified candidates for appointment or assignment in such capacity.

PART B—FOREIGN SERVICE OFFICERS

APPOINTMENTS

SEC. 511. The President shall appoint Foreign Service officers by and with the advice and consent of the Senate. All appointments of Foreign Service officers shall be by appointment to a class and not to a particular post.

COMMISSIONS

SEC. 512. Foreign Service officers may be commissioned as diplomatic or consular officers or both and all official acts of such officers while serving under diplomatic or consular commissions shall be performed under their respective commissions as diplomatic or consular officers.

LIMITS OF CONSULAR DISTRICTS

SEC. 513. The Secretary shall define the limits of consular districts.

ASSIGNMENTS AND TRANSFERS

SEC. 514. A Foreign Service officer, commissioned as a diplomatic or consular officer, may be assigned by the Secretary to serve in any diplomatic position other than that of chief of mission or in any consular position, and he may also be assigned to serve in any other capacity in which he is eligible to serve under the terms of this or any other Act. He may be transferred from one post to another by order of the Secretary as the interests of the Service may require.

CITIZENSHIP REQUIREMENTS

SEC. 515. No person shall be eligible for appointment as a Foreign Service officer unless he is a citizen of the United States and has been such for at least ten years.

ADMISSION TO CLASS 6

SEC. 516. No person shall be eligible for appointment as a Foreign Service officer of class 6 unless he has passed such written, oral, physical, and other examinations as the Board of Examiners for the Foreign Service may prescribe to determine his fitness and aptitude for the work of the Service and has demonstrated his loyalty to the Government of the United States and his attachment to the principles of the Constitution. The Secretary shall furnish the President with the names of those persons who have passed such examinations and are eligible for appointment as Foreign Service officers of class 6.

ADMISSION TO CLASSES 1, 2, 3, 4, AND 5 WITHOUT PRIOR SERVICE IN CLASS 6

SEC. 517. A person who has not served in class 6 shall not be eligible for appointment as a Foreign Service officer of classes 1 to 5, inclusive, unless he has passed such written, oral, physical, and other examinations as the Board of Examiners for the Foreign Service may prescribe to determine his fitness and aptitude for the work of the Service; demonstrated his loyalty to the Government of the United States and his attachment to the principles of the Constitution; and rendered at least four years of actual service immediately prior to appointment in a position of responsibility in the Service or in the Department or both, except that, if he has reached the age of thirty-one years, the requirement as to service may be reduced to three years. The Secretary shall furnish the President with the names of those persons who shall have passed such examinations and are eligible for appointment as Foreign Service officers of classes 1 to 5, inclusive. The Secretary shall, taking into consideration the age, qualifications, and experience of each candidate for appointment, recommend the class to which he shall be appointed in accordance with the provisions of this section.

ADMISSION TO THE CLASS OF CAREER MINISTER

SEC. 518. No person shall be eligible for appointment to the class of career minister who is not a Foreign Service officer.

REASSIGNMENT TO FOREIGN SERVICE OF FORMER AMBASSADORS AND MINISTERS

SEC. 519. If, within three months of the date of the termination of his services as chief of mission and of any period of authorized leave, a Foreign Service officer has not again been appointed or assigned as chief of mission or assigned in accordance with the provisions of section 514, he shall be retired from the Service and receive retirement benefits in accordance with the provisions of section 821.

REINSTATEMENT AND RECALL OF FOREIGN SERVICE OFFICERS

SEC. 520. (a) The President may, by and with the advice and consent of the Senate, reappoint to the Service a former Foreign Service officer who has been separated from the Service by reason of appointment to some other position in the Government service and who has served continuously in the Government up to the time of reinstatement. The Secretary shall, taking into consideration the qualifications and experience of each candidate for reappointment and the rank of his contemporaries in the Service, recommend the class to which he shall be reappointed in accordance with the provisions of this section.

(b) Whenever the Secretary shall determine an emergency to exist, the Secretary may recall any retired Foreign Service officer temporarily to active service.

PART C—FOREIGN SERVICE RESERVE OFFICERS

ESTABLISHMENT OF RESERVE

SEC. 521. In accordance with the terms of this Act and under such regulations as the Secretary shall prescribe, there shall be organized and maintained a Foreign Service Reserve, referred to hereafter as the Reserve.

APPOINTMENTS AND ASSIGNMENTS TO THE RESERVE

SEC. 522. Whenever the services of a person who is a citizen of the United States and who has been such for at least five years are required by the Service, the Secretary may—

(1) appoint as a Reserve officer for nonconsecutive periods of not more than four years each, a person not in the employ of the Government whom the Board of the Foreign Service shall deem to have outstanding qualifications of a specialized character; and

(2) assign as a Reserve officer for nonconsecutive periods of not more than four years each a person regularly employed in any Government agency, subject, in the case of an employee of a Government agency other than the Department of State, to the consent of the head of the agency concerned.

APPOINTMENT OR ASSIGNMENT TO A CLASS

SEC. 523. A Reserve officer, appointed or assigned to active duty, shall be appointed or assigned to a class and not to a particular post, and such an officer may be assigned to posts and may be transferred from one post to another by order of the Secretary as the interests of the Service may require. The class to which he shall be appointed or assigned shall depend on his age, qualifications, and experience.

COMMISSIONS

SEC. 524. Whenever the Secretary shall deem it in the interests of the Service that a Reserve officer shall serve in a diplomatic or consular capacity, he may recommend to the President that such officer be commissioned as a diplomatic or consular officer or both. The President may, by and with the advice and consent of the Senate, commission such officer as a diplomatic or consular officer or both, and all official acts of such an officer while serving under a diplomatic or consular commission shall be performed under his commission as a diplomatic or consular officer. In all other cases, appropriate rank and status, analogous to that of Foreign Service officers engaged in work of comparable importance shall be provided to permit Reserve officers to carry out their duties effectively.

ACTIVE DUTY

SEC. 525. The Secretary shall by regulation define the period during which a Reserve officer shall be considered as being on active duty.

BENEFITS

SEC. 526. A Reserve officer shall, except as otherwise provided in regulations which the Secretary may prescribe, receive all the allowances, privileges, and benefits which Foreign Service officers are entitled to receive in accordance with the provisions of title IX.

REAPPOINTMENT OR REASSIGNMENT OF RESERVE OFFICERS

SEC. 527. A person who has served as a Reserve officer may not be reappointed or reassigned to active duty until the expiration of a period of time equal to his preceding tour of duty or until the expiration of a year, whichever is the shorter.

REINSTATEMENT OF RESERVE OFFICERS

SEC. 528. Upon the termination of the assignment of a Reserve officer assigned from any Government agency, such person shall be entitled to reinstatement in the Government agency by which he is regularly employed in the same position he occupied at the time of assignment, or in a corresponding or higher position. Upon reinstatement he shall receive the within-grade salary advancements he would have been entitled to receive had he remained in the position in which he is regularly employed under subsection (d), section 7, of the Classification Act of 1923, as amended, or any corresponding provision of law applicable to the position in which he is serving. A certificate of the Secretary that such person has met the standards required for the efficient conduct of the work of the Foreign Service shall satisfy any requirements as to the holding of minimum ratings as a prerequisite to the receipt of such salary advancements.

Part D—Foreign Service Staff Officers and Employees

APPOINTMENTS

Sec. 531. The Secretary shall appoint staff officers and employees under such regulations as he may prescribe and, as soon as practicable, in accordance with the provisions of sections 441, 442, and 443.

ASSIGNMENTS AND TRANSFERS

Sec. 532. The Secretary may, in accordance with uniform procedures established in such regulations as he may prescribe, assign a staff officer or employee to a position at any post and transfer such a person from a position in one class to a vacant position within the same class, and from one post to another. Upon demonstration of ability to assume duties of greater responsibility, such person may, as provided in section 641, be promoted to a vacant position in a higher class at the same or at a higher rate of salary and he may be transferred from one post to another in connection with such promotion.

COMMISSION AS CONSUL OR VICE CONSUL

Sec. 533. On the recommendation of the Secretary, the President may, by and with the advice and consent of the Senate, commission a staff officer or employee as consul. The Secretary may commission a staff officer or employee as vice consul. Official acts of staff officers or employees while serving under consular commissions in the Service shall be performed under their respective commissions as consular officers.

CITIZENSHIP REQUIREMENT

Sec. 534. No person shall be eligible for appointment as staff officer or employee who is not a citizen of the United States at the time of his appointment.

Part E—Alien Clerks and Employees
APPOINTMENTS

Sec. 541. The Secretary shall appoint alien clerks and employees at posts abroad under such regulations as he may prescribe and, as soon as practicable, in accordance with the provisions of section 444.

ASSIGNMENTS AND TRANSFERS

SEC. 542. The Secretary may assign an alien clerk or employee to a position at any post, and any such clerk or employee may be transferred from a position at one post to a position at another as the interests of the Service may require.

PART F—CONSULAR AGENTS

SEC. 551. The Secretary may appoint consular agents under such regulations as he may prescribe and, as soon as practicable, in accordance with the provisions of section 445.

PART G—ASSIGNMENT OF PERSONNEL BY THE WAR AND NAVY DEPARTMENTS

AS COURIERS AND INSPECTORS OF BUILDINGS

SEC. 561. The Secretaries of War and Navy are authorized, upon the request of the Secretary, to assign or detail military and naval personnel serving under their supervision for duty as inspectors of buildings owned or occupied abroad by the United States or as inspectors or supervisors of buildings under construction or repair abroad by or for the United States, or for duty as couriers of the Department; and, when so assigned or detailed, they may receive the same traveling expenses as are authorized for officers of the Service, payable from applicable appropriations of the Department. Such assignments or details may, in the discretion of the head of the department concerned, be made without reimbursement from the Department of State.

AS CUSTODIANS

SEC. 562. The Secretary of the Navy is authorized, upon request of the Secretary of State, to assign enlisted men of the Navy and the Marine Corps to serve as custodians under the supervision of the principal officer at an embassy, legation, or consulate.

PART H—ASSIGNMENT OF FOREIGN SERVICE PERSONNEL
ASSIGNMENTS TO ANY GOVERNMENT AGENCY

SEC. 571. (a) Any officer or employee of the Service may, in the discretion of the Director General, be assigned or detailed for duty in any Government agency, such an assignment or combination of assignments to be for a period of not more than four years. He may not again be assigned for duty in a Government agency until the expiration of a period of time equal to his preceding tour of duty on such assignment or until the expiration of two years, whichever is the shorter.

(b) A Foreign Service officer may be appointed as Director General or Deputy Director General, notwithstanding the provisions of the last sentence of paragraph (a) of this section, but any such officer may not serve longer than four years in such position or positions and upon the completion of such service may not again be assigned to a position in the Department until the expiration of a period of time equal to his tour of duty as Director General or Deputy Director General or until the expiration of two years, whichever is shorter.

(c) If a Foreign Service officer shall be appointed by the President, by and with the advice and consent of the Senate, to a position in the Department, the period of his service in such capacity shall be construed as constituting an assignment for duty in the Department within the meaning of paragraph (a) of this section and such person shall not, by virtue of the acceptance of such an assignment, lose his status as a Foreign Service officer. Service in such a position shall not, however, be subject to the limitations concerning the duration of an assignment or concerning reassignment contained in that paragraph.

(d) If the basic minimum salary of the position to which an officer or employee of the Service is assigned pursuant to the terms of this section is higher than the salary such officer or employee is entitled to receive as an officer or employee of the Service, such officer or employee shall, during the period such difference in salary exists, receive the salary of the position in which he is serving in lieu of his salary as an officer or employee of the Service. Any salary paid under the provisions of this section shall be paid from appropriations made available for the payment of salaries of officers and employees of the Service and shall be the salary on the basis of which computations and payments shall be made in accordance with the provisions of title VIII.

COMPULSORY SERVICE OF FOREIGN SERVICE OFFICERS IN THE CONTINENTAL UNITED STATES

SEC. 572. Every Foreign Service officer shall, during his first fifteen years of service in such capacity, be assigned for duty in the continental United States in accordance with the provisions of section 571 for periods totaling not less than three years.

ASSIGNMENT FOR CONSULTATION OR INSTRUCTION

SEC. 573. (a) Any officer or employee of the Service may, in the discretion of the Secretary, be assigned or detailed to any Government agency for consultation or specific instruction either at the commencement, during the course of, or at the close of the period of his official service; and any such detail or assignment, if not more than four months in duration, shall not be considered as an assignment within the meaning of section 571.

(b) Any officer or employee of the Service may be assigned or detailed for special instruction or training at or with public or private nonprofit institutions; trade, labor, agricultural, or scientific associations; or commercial firms.

ASSIGNMENT TO TRADE, LABOR, AGRICULTURAL, SCIENTIFIC, OR OTHER CONFERENCES

SEC. 574. An officer or employee of the Service may, in the discretion of the Secretary, be assigned, or detailed for duty with domestic or international trade, labor, agricultural, scientific, or other conferences, congresses, or gatherings, including those whose place of meeting is in the continental United States; or for other special duties, including temporary details under commission not at his post or in the Department.

ASSIGNMENTS TO FOREIGN GOVERNMENTS

SEC. 575. The Secretary may, in his discretion, assign or detail an officer or employee of the Service for temporary service to or in cooperation with the government of another country in accordance with the provisions of the Act of May 25, 1938, as amended (52 Stat. 442; 53 Stat. 652; 5 U. S. C. 118e).

ASSIGNMENTS TO INTERNATIONAL ORGANIZATIONS

SEC. 576. The Secretary may, in his discretion, assign or detail an officer or employee of the Service for temporary service to or in cooperation with an international organization in which the United States participates under the same conditions as those governing the assignment or detail of officers or employees of the Service to the government of another country in accordance with the provisions of the Act of May 25, 1938, as amended (52 Stat. 442; 53 Stat. 652; 5 U. S. C. 118e).

ASSIGNMENT OR DETAIL TO THE UNITED STATES NOT TO AFFECT PERSONNEL CEILINGS

SEC. 577. An officer or employee of the Service assigned or detailed to the continental United States in accordance with the provisions of this Act shall not be counted as a civilian employee within the meaning of section 607 of the Federal Employees' Pay Act of 1945, as amended by section 14 of the Federal Employees' Pay Act of 1946.

TITLE VI—PERSONNEL ADMINISTRATION

PART A—DEFINITIONS

SEC. 601. For the purpose of this title—

(1) "Efficiency record" is the term which describes those materials considered by the Director General to be pertinent to the preparation of an evaluation of the performance of an officer or employee of the Service.

(2) "Efficiency report" is the term which designates the analysis of the performance of an officer or employee made by his supervising officer or by a Foreign Service inspector in accordance with such regulations as may be prescribed by the Secretary.

[179]

Part B—Efficiency Records

RESPONSIBILITY OF THE DIRECTOR GENERAL FOR THE KEEPING OF EFFICIENCY RECORDS

SEC. 611. The Director General, acting under the general direction of the Board of the Foreign Service, shall be responsible for the keeping of accurate and impartial efficiency records. Under his direction there shall be assembled, recorded, and preserved all available information in regard to the character, ability, conduct, quality of work, industry, experience, dependability, and general usefulness of all officers and employees of the Service, including the reports of Foreign Service inspectors and the efficiency reports of supervising officers. The Director General shall undertake such statistical and other analyses as may be necessary to develop the validity and reliability of efficiency reporting forms and procedures.

TO WHOM RECORDS SHALL BE AVAILABLE

SEC. 612. The correspondence and records of the Department relating to the officers and employees of the Service, including efficiency records as defined in section 601 (1) but not including records pertaining to the receipt, disbursement, and accounting for public funds, shall be confidential and subject to inspection only by the President, the Secretary, the Under Secretary, the Counselor of the Department, the legislative and appropriations committees of the Congress charged with considering legislation and appropriations for the Service or representatives duly authorized by such committees, the members of the Board of the Foreign Service, the Director General, and such officers and employees of the Government as may be assigned by the Secretary to work on such records. Under such regulations as the Secretary may prescribe and in the interest of efficient personnel administration, the whole or any portion of an efficiency record shall, upon written requests, be divulged to the officer or employee to whom such record relates.

Part C—Promotion of Foreign Service Officers and Foreign Service Reserve Officers

PROMOTION OF FOREIGN SERVICE OFFICERS BY SELECTION

SEC. 621. All promotions of Foreign Service officers shall be made by the President, in accordance with such regulations as he may prescribe, by appointment to a higher class, by and with the advice and consent of the Senate. Promotion shall be by selection on the basis of merit.

ELIGIBILITY

SEC. 622. The Secretary shall, by regulation, determine the minimum period Foreign Service officers must serve in each class and a standard for performance for each class which they must meet in order to become eligible for promotion to a higher class. In the event the Director General shall certify to the Board of the Foreign Service that a Foreign Service officer has rendered extraordinarily meritorious service, the Board of the Foreign Service may recommend to the Secretary that such officer shall not be required to serve such minimum period in class as a prerequisite to promotion, and the Secretary may exempt such officer from such requirement.

RECOMMENDATIONS FOR PROMOTION

SEC. 623. The Secretary is authorized to establish, with the advice of the Board of the Foreign Service, selection boards to evaluate the performance of Foreign Service officers, and upon the basis of their findings the Secretary shall make recommendations to the President for the promotion of Foreign Service officers. No person assigned to serve on any such board shall serve in such capacity for any two consecutive years.

PROMOTION OF FOREIGN SERVICE RESERVE OFFICERS

SEC. 624. Any Reserve officer may receive promotions from one class to a next higher class in accordance with regulations prescribed by the Secretary.

[181]

IN-CLASS PROMOTIONS OF FOREIGN SERVICE OFFICERS AND RESERVE OFFICERS

SEC. 625. Any Foreign Service officer or any Reserve officer, whose services meet the standards required for the efficient conduct of the work of the Foreign Service and who shall have been in a given class for a continuous period of nine months or more, shall, on the first day of each fiscal year, receive an increase in salary to the next higher rate for the class in which he is serving. The Secretary is authorized to grant to a Foreign Service officer or a Reserve officer, in any class, additional increases in salary within the salary range established for the class in which he is serving, based upon especially meritorious service.

PART D—SEPARATION OF FOREIGN SERVICE OFFICERS FROM THE SERVICE

FOREIGN SERVICE OFFICERS WHO ARE CAREER MINISTERS

SEC. 631. Any Foreign Service officer who is a career minister, other than one occupying a position as chief of mission, shall, upon reaching the age of sixty-five, be retired from the Service and receive retirement benefits in accordance with the provisions of section 821, but whenever the Secretary shall determine an emergency to exist, he may, in the public interest, extend such an officer's service for a period not to exceed five years.

FOREIGN SERVICE OFFICERS WHO ARE NOT CAREER MINISTERS

SEC. 632. Any Foreign Service officer who is not a career minister shall, upon reaching the age of sixty, be retired from the Service and receive retirement benefits in accordance with the provisions of section 821 but when the Secretary shall determine an emergency to exist, he may, in the public interest, extend such an officer's service for a period not to exceed five years.

FOREIGN SERVICE OFFICERS IN CLASSES 2 AND 3

SEC. 633. The Secretary shall prescribe the maximum period during which Foreign Service officers in classes 2 or 3 shall be permitted to remain in such classes without promotion. Any officer who does not receive a promotion to a higher class within that period shall be retired from the Service and receive retirement benefits in accordance with the provisions of section 821.

FOREIGN SERVICE OFFICERS IN CLASSES 4 AND 5

SEC. 634. (a) The Secretary shall prescribe the maximum period during which Foreign Service officers in classes 4 or 5 shall be permitted to remain in such classes without promotion. Any officer who does not receive a promotion to a higher class within that period shall be retired from the Service and receive benefits as follows:

(1) One-twelfth of a year's salary at his then current salary rate for each year of service and proportionately for a fraction of a year, payable without interest, in three equal installments on the 1st day of January following the officer's retirement and on the two anniversaries of this date immediately following; and

(2) A refund of the contributions made to the Foreign Service Retirement and Disability Fund, with interest thereon at 4 per centum, compounded annually, except that in lieu of such refund such officer may elect to receive retirement benefits on reaching the age of sixty-two, in accordance with the provisions of section 821. In the event that an officer who was separated from class 4 and who has elected to receive retirement benefits dies before reaching the age of sixty-two, his death shall be considered a death in service within the meaning of section 832. In the event that an officer who was separated from class 5 and who has elected to receive retirement benefits dies before reaching the age of sixty-two, the total amount of his contributions made to the Foreign Service Retirement and Disability Fund, with interest thereon at 4 per centum, compounded annually, shall be paid in accordance with the provisions of section 841.

(b) Notwithstanding the provisions of section 3477 of the Revised Statutes (31 U. S. C. 203) or the provisions of any other law, a Foreign Service officer who is retired in accordance with the provisions of this section shall have the right to assign to any person or corporation the whole or any part of the benefits receivable by him pursuant to paragraph (a) (1) of this section. Any such assignment shall be on a form approved by the Secretary of the Treasury and a copy thereof shall be deposited with the Secretary of the Treasury by the officer executing the assignment.

FOREIGN SERVICE OFFICERS RETIRED FROM CLASS 6

SEC. 635. Any Foreign Service officer in class 6 shall occupy probationary status. The Secretary may terminate his service at any time.

VOLUNTARY RETIREMENT

SEC. 636. Any Foreign Service officer who is at least fifty years of age and has rendered twenty years of service, including service within the meaning of section 853, may on his own application and with the consent of the Secretary be retired from the Service and receive benefits in accordance with the provisions of section 821.

SEPARATION FOR UNSATISFACTORY PERFORMANCE OF DUTY

SEC. 637. (a) The Secretary may, under such regulations as he may prescribe, separate from the Service any Foreign Service officer above class 6 on account of the unsatisfactory performance of his duties; but no such officer shall be so separated from the Service until he shall have been granted a hearing by the Board of the Foreign Service and the unsatisfactory performance of his duties shall have been established at such hearing.

(b) Any Foreign Service officer over forty-five years of age, separated from the Service in accordance with the provisions of paragraph (a) of this section, shall be retired upon an annuity computed in accordance with the provisions of section 821 but not in excess of 25 per centum of his per annum salary at the time of his separation.

(c) Any Foreign Service officer under forty-five years of age, separated from the Service in accordance with the provisions of paragraph (a) of this section, shall at the time of separation receive a payment equal to one year's salary or the refund of the contributions made by him to the Foreign Service Retirement and Disability Fund, whichever shall be greater.

(d) Any payments made in accordance with the provisions of

this section shall be made out of the Foreign Service Retirement and Disability Fund.

SEPARATION FOR MISCONDUCT OR MALFEASANCE

SEC. 638. The Secretary shall separate from the Service any Foreign Service officer or Reserve officer who shall be guilty of misconduct or malfeasance in office, but no such officer shall be so separated from the Service until he shall have been granted a hearing by the Board of the Foreign Service and his misconduct or malfeasance shall have been established at such hearing. Any officer separated from the Service in accordance with the provisions of this section shall not be eligible to receive the benefits provided by title VIII of this Act, but his contributions to the Foreign Service Retirement and Disability Fund shall be returned to him in accordance with the provisions of section 841 (a).

PART E—PROMOTION OF FOREIGN SERVICE STAFF OFFICERS AND EMPLOYEES

CLASS PROMOTION OF STAFF PERSONNEL

SEC. 641. Any staff officer or employee may, in accordance with uniform procedures established in regulations prescribed by the Secretary, upon demonstration of ability to assume duties of greater responsibility, be promoted to a vacant position in a higher class at the same or at a higher rate of salary.

IN-CLASS PROMOTIONS OF STAFF OFFICERS AND EMPLOYEES

SEC. 642. In-class promotions of staff officers and employees shall be granted in accordance with regulations prescribed by the Secretary.

PART F—SEPARATION OF STAFF OFFICERS AND EMPLOYEES

FOR UNSATISFACTORY PERFORMANCE OF DUTY

SEC. 651. The Secretary may, under such regulations as he may prescribe, separate from the Service any staff officer or employee on account of the unsatisfactory performance of his duties, but no such officer or employee shall be so separated from the Service until he shall have been granted a hearing by the Board of the Foreign Service and the unsatisfactory performance of his duties shall have been established at such hearing.

FOR MISCONDUCT OR MALFEASANCE

SEC. 652. The Secretary shall separate from the Service any staff officer or employee who shall be guilty of misconduct or malfeasance in office, but no such officer or employee shall be so separated from the Service until he shall have been granted a hearing by the Board of the Foreign Service and his misconduct or malfeasance shall have been established at such hearing.

PART G—PROMOTION AND SEPARATION OF ALIEN CLERKS AND EMPLOYEES

PROMOTION

SEC. 661. Alien clerks and employees shall receive promotions from one class to a higher class and in-class promotions in accordance with regulations prescribed by the Secretary.

FOR UNSATISFACTORY PERFORMANCE OF DUTY

SEC. 662. The Secretary may, under such regulations as he may prescribe, separate from the Service any alien clerk or employee on account of the unsatisfactory performance of his duties.

SEPARATION FOR MISCONDUCT OR MALFEASANCE

SEC. 663. The Secretary shall separate from the Service any alien clerk or employee who shall be found guilty of misconduct or malfeasance.

PART H—SEPARATION OF CONSULAR AGENTS

SEC. 671. The Secretary may, under such regulations as he may prescribe, separate any consular agent from the Service on account of—

(a) the unsatisfactory performance of his duties; or
(b) misconduct or malfeasance.

PART I—INSPECTIONS

SEC. 681. The Secretary shall assign or detail Foreign Service officers as Foreign Service inspectors to inspect in a substantially uniform manner and at least once every two years the work of the diplomatic and consular establishments of the United States. Whenever the Secretary has reason to believe that the business of a consulate is not being properly conducted and that it is necessary in the public interest, he may authorize any Foreign Service inspector to suspend the principal officer or any subordinate consular officer and to administer the office in the place of the principal officer for a period not exceeding ninety days. The Secretary may also authorize a Foreign Service inspector to suspend any diplomatic officer except a chief of mission. A Foreign Service inspector shall have the authority to suspend any other officer or employee of the Service.

TITLE VII—THE FOREIGN SERVICE INSTITUTE

ESTABLISHMENT OF THE INSTITUTE

SEC. 701. The Secretary shall, in order to furnish training and instruction to officers and employees of the Service and of the Department and to other officers and employees of the Government for whom training and instruction in the field of foreign relations is necessary, and in order to promote and foster programs of study incidental to such training, establish a Foreign Service Institute, hereinafter called the Institute.

THE DIRECTOR OF THE INSTITUTE—APPOINTMENT, SALARY, AND DUTIES

SEC. 702. The head of the Institute, who shall be known as its Director, shall be appointed by the Secretary. The Director shall, under the general supervision of the Director General and under such regulations as the Secretary may prescribe, establish the basic procedures to be followed by the Institute; plan and provide for the general nature of the training and instruction to be furnished at the Institute; correlate the training and instruction to be furnished at the Institute with the training activities of the Department and other Government agencies and with courses given at private institutions that are designed or may serve to furnish training and instruction to officers and employees of the Service; encourage and foster such programs outside of the Institute as will be complementary to those of the Institute; and take such other action as may be required for the proper administration of the Institute.

AID TO NONPROFIT INSTITUTIONS

SEC. 703. The Secretary may, within the limits of such appropriations as may be made specifically therefor, make grants or furnish such other gratuitous assistance as he may deem necessary or advisable to nonprofit institutions cooperating with the Institute in any of the programs conducted by the Director by authority of this title.

APPOINTMENT, ASSIGNMENT, AND DETAIL TO THE INSTITUTE

SEC. 704. (a) The Secretary may appoint to the faculty or staff of the Institute on a full- or part-time basis such personnel as he may deem necessary to carry out the provisions of this title in accordance with the provisions of the civil-service laws and regulations and the Classification Act of 1923, as amended, except that, when deemed necessary by the Secretary for the effective administration of this title, personnel may be appointed without regard to such laws and regulations, but any person so appointed shall receive a salary at one of the rates provided by the Classification Act of 1923, as amended. All appointments to the faculty or staff of the Institute shall be made without regard to political affiliations and shall be made solely on the basis of demonstrated interest in, and capacity to promote, the purposes of the Institute.

(b) The Secretary may, under such regulations as he may prescribe and on a full- or part-time basis, assign or detail officers and employees of the Service to serve on the faculty or staff of the Institute or to receive training at the Institute.

(c) The Secretary may, under such regulations as he may prescribe and on a full- or part-time basis, assign or detail any officer or employee of the Department, and, with the consent of the head of the Government agency concerned, any other officer or employee of the Government, to serve on the faculty or staff of the Institute, or to receive training. During the period of his assignment or detail, such officer or employee shall be considered as remaining in the position from which assigned.

(d) It shall be the duty of the Director to make recommendations to the Secretary with regard to the appointment, assignment, or detail of persons to serve on the faculty or staff of the Institute, and the Secretary shall in each case take such recommendations into consideration in making such appointments, assignments, or details.

INSTRUCTION AND EDUCATION AT OTHER LOCALITIES THAN THE INSTITUTE

SEC. 705. The Secretary may, under such regulations as he may prescribe, pay the tuition and other expenses of officers and employees of the Service, assigned or detailed in accordance with the provisions of section 573 (b) for special instruction or training at or with public or private nonprofit institutions, trade, labor, agricultural, or scientific associations, or commercial firms.

ENDOWMENTS AND GIFTS TO THE INSTITUTE

SEC. 706. The Secretary may accept, receive, hold, and administer gifts, bequests, or devises of money, securities, or property made for the benefit of, or in connection with, the Foreign Service Institute in accordance with part C of title X.

ACQUISITION OF REAL PROPERTY FOR THE INSTITUTE

SEC. 707. The Secretary may, in the name of the United States, acquire such real property as may be necessary for the operation and maintenance of the Institute and, without regard to section 3709 of the Revised Statutes, such other property and equipment as may be necessary for its operation and maintenance.

TITLE VIII—THE FOREIGN SERVICE RETIREMENT AND DISABILITY SYSTEM

PART A—ESTABLISHMENT OF SYSTEM

RULES AND REGULATIONS

SEC. 801. (a) The President may prescribe rules and regulations for the maintenance of a Foreign Service Retirement and

[189]

Disability System, originally established by section 18 of the Act of May 24, 1924 (43 Stat. 144), referred to hereafter as the System.

(b) The Secretary shall administer the System in accordance with such rules and regulations and with the principles established by this Act.

MAINTENANCE OF FUND

SEC. 802. The Secretary of the Treasury shall maintain the special fund, known as the Foreign Service Retirement and Disability Fund, referred to hereafter as the Fund, originally constituted by section 18 of the Act of May 24, 1924 (43 Stat. 144).

PARTICIPANTS

SEC. 803. (a) The following persons, hereafter referred to as participants, shall be entitled to the benefits of the System:

(1) All Foreign Service officers;

(2) All other persons making contributions to the Fund on the effective date of this Act;

(3) Any chief of mission who is not otherwise entitled to be a participant and who fulfills the conditions of paragraph (b) of this section;

(b) A person to become a participant in accordance with the provisions of paragraphs (a) (3) of this section must—

(1) have served as chief of mission for an aggregate period of twenty years or more, exclusive of extra service credit in accordance with the provisions of section 853; and

(2) have paid into the Fund a special contribution equal to 5 per centum of his basic salary for each year of such service with interest thereon to date of payment, compounded annually at 4 per centum.

ANNUITANTS

SEC. 804. Annuitants shall be persons who are receiving annuities from the Fund on the effective date of this Act, persons who shall become entitled to receive annuities in accordance with the provisions of sections 519, 631, 632, 633, 634, 636, 637, 831, 832, and 833, and all widows and beneficiaries of participants who are entitled to receive annuities in accordance with the terms of this title.

Part B—Compulsory Contributions

Sec. 811. (a) Five per centum of the basic salary of all participants shall be contributed to the Fund, and the Secretary of the Treasury is directed to cause such deductions to be made and the sums transferred on the books of the Treasury Department to the credit of the Fund for the payment of annuities, cash benefits, refunds, and allowances.

(b) All basic salaries in excess of $13,500 per annum shall be treated as $13,500 for the purposes of this title.

Part C—Computation of Annuities

Sec. 821. (a) The annuity of a participant shall be equal to 2 per centum of his average basic salary, not exceeding $13,500 per annum, for the five years next preceding the date of his retirement multiplied by the number of years of service, not exceeding thirty years. In determining the aggregate period of service upon which the annuity is to be based, the fractional part of a month, if any, shall not be counted.

(b) At the time of his retirement, a participant, if the husband of a wife to whom he has been married for at least three years or who is the mother of issue by such marriage, may elect to receive a reduced annuity for himself and to provide for an annuity payable to his widow, commencing on the date following his death and continuing as long as she may live. The annuity payable to his widow shall in no case exceed 25 per centum of his average basic salary for the five years next preceding his retirement or $66\frac{2}{3}$ per centum of his reduced annuity. If the age of the participant is less than the age of the wife or exceeds her age by not more than eight years, the annuity of the participant will be reduced by an amount equal to one-half of the annuity which he elects to have paid to his widow. If the age of the participant exceeds the age of the wife by more than eight years, the annuity of the participant will be reduced by an amount equal to one-half the annuity which he elects to have paid to his widow plus an additional reduction equal to 2 per centum of such widow's annuity for each year, or fraction thereof, that the difference in age exceeds eight. The participant may at his option also elect to have his annuity reduced by an additional 5 per centum of the amount which he elects to have paid to his widow, with a provision that, from and after the death of his wife, if the participant shall survive her, the annuity payable to the participant shall be that amount which would have been payable if no option had been elected.

(c) A participant who is not married at the time of his retirement or who is married to a wife who is not entitled to an annuity in accordance with the provisions of paragraph (b) of this section may elect to receive a reduced annuity for himself and to provide for an additional annuity payable after his death to a beneficiary whose name shall be notified in writing to the Secretary at the time of his retirement and who is acceptable to the Secretary. The annuity payments payable to such beneficiary shall be either equal to the deceased participant's reduced annuity payments or equal to 50 per centum of such reduced annuity payments and upon the death of the surviving beneficiary all payments shall cease and no further annuity payments shall be due or payable. The combined actuarial value of the two annuities on the date of retirement as determined by the Secretary of the Treasury shall be the same as the actuarial value of the annuity provided by paragraph (a) of this section. No such election of a reduced annuity payable to a beneficiary other than a child of the participant shall be valid until the participant shall have satisfactorily passed a physical examination as prescribed by the Secretary. Annuity payments payable in accordance with the provisions of this section to a beneficiary who is a child of a participant shall cease when the beneficiary reaches the age of twenty-one years.

Part D—Benefits Accruing to Certain Participants

RETIREMENT FOR DISABILITY OR INCAPACITY—PHYSICAL EXAMINATION —RECOVERY

SEC. 831. (a) Any participant who, after serving for a total period of not less than five years, becomes totally disabled or incapacitated for useful and efficient service by reason of disease or injury incurred in the line of duty but not due to vicious habits, intemperance, or willful misconduct on his part, shall, upon his own application or upon order of the Secretary, be retired on an annuity computed as prescribed in section 821. If the disabled or incapacitated participant has had less than twenty years of service at the time he is retired, his annuity shall be computed on the assumption that he had had twenty years of service.

(b) In each case such disability shall be determined by the report of a duly qualified physician or surgeon, designated by the Secretary to conduct the examination. Unless the disability is permanent, a like examination shall be made annually until the annuitant has reached the retirement age as defined in sections 631 and 632, and the payment of the annuity shall cease from the date of a medical examination showing recovery. Fees for examinations under this provision, together with reasonable traveling and other expenses incurred in order to submit to examination, shall be paid out of the Fund.

(c) When the annuity is discontinued under this provision before the annuitant has received a sum equal to the total amount of his contributions, with accrued interest, the difference shall be paid to him or his legal representatives in the order of precedence prescribed in section 841.

DEATH IN SERVICE

SEC. 832. In case a participant shall die without having established a valid claim for annuity, the total amount of his contributions with interest thereon at 4 per centum per annum, compounded on June 30 of each year, except as provided in section 881 and as hereinafter provided in this section, shall be paid to his legal representatives in the order of precedence given under section 841 upon the establishment of a valid claim therefor. If the deceased participant rendered at least five years of service, and is survived by a widow to whom he was married for at least three years, or who is the mother of issue by such marriage, such widow shall be paid an annuity equal to the annuity which she would have been entitled to receive if her husband had been retired on the date of his death and had elected to receive a reduced joint and survivorship annuity, computed as prescribed in section 821, providing the maximum annuity for his widow, unless prior to the date of his death he shall have elected, in lieu of such widow's annuity, and with the approval of the Secretary, to have his deductions returned with interest as provided in the first sentence of this section covering participants dying without having established a valid claim for annuity. If the deceased participant had had less than twenty years of service at the time of his death, the annuity payable to his widow shall be computed on the assumption that he had had twenty years of service.

RETIREMENT OF PERSONS WHO ARE PARTICIPANTS UNDER SECTION 803 (A) (3)

SEC. 833. (a) Any person who is a participant, has at least twenty years of service to his credit, and has reached the age of fifty years, but is not a Foreign Service officer at the time he is retired in accordance with the provisions of law governing retirement in the position that he occupies, shall be entitled to an annuity computed as prescribed in section 821.

(b) Any person who is a participant in accordance with the provisions of section 803 (a) (3) shall be entitled to voluntary retirement to the same extent and subject to the same conditions as a Foreign Service officer.

PART E—DISPOSITION OF CONTRIBUTIONS AND INTEREST IN EXCESS OF BENEFITS RECEIVED

SEC. 841. (a) Whenever a participant becomes separated from the Service without becoming eligible for an annuity or a deferred annuity in accordance with the provisions of this Act, the total amount of contributions from his salary with interest thereon at 4 per centum per annum, compounded annually up to the date of such separation, except as provided in section 881, shall be returned to him.

(b) In the event that the total contributions of a retired participant, other than voluntary contributions made in accordance with the provisions of section 881, with interest compounded annually at 4 per centum added thereto, exceed the total amount returned to such participant or to an annuitant claiming through him, in the form of annuities, accumulated at the same rate of interest up to the date the annuity payments cease under the terms of the annuity, the excess of the accumulated contributions over the accumulated annuity payments shall be paid in the following

[194]

order of precedence, upon the establishment of a valid claim therefor:

(1) To the beneficiary or beneficiaries designated by the retired participant in writing to the Secretary;

(2) If there be no such beneficiary, to the duly appointed executor or administrator of the estate of the retired participant;

(3) If there be no such beneficiary, or executor or administrator, payment may be made to such person or persons as may appear in the judgment of the Secretary to be legally entitled thereto, and such payment shall be a ban to recovery by any other person.

(c) No payment shall be made pursuant to paragraph (b) (3) of this section until after the expiration of thirty days from the death of the retired participant or his surviving annuitant.

Part F—Period of Service for Annuities

COMPUTATION OF LENGTH OF SERVICE

SEC. 851. For the purposes of this title, the period of service of a participant shall be computed from the effective date of appointment as Foreign Service officer, or, if appointed prior to July 1, 1924, as diplomatic secretary, consul general, consul, vice consul, deputy consul, consular assistant, consular agent, commercial agent, interpreter, or student interpreter, and shall include periods of service at different times as either a diplomatic or consular officer, or while on assignment to the Department, or while on special duty or service in another department or establishment of the Government, or while on any assignment in accordance with the provisions of part H of title V, but all periods of separation from the Service and so much of any leaves of absence as may exceed six months in the aggregate in any calendar year shall be excluded, except sick leaves of absence for illness or injury incurred in the line of duty, with or without pay, and leaves of absences granted participants while performing active military or naval service in the Army, Navy, Marine Corps, or Coast Guard of the United States.

PRIOR SERVICE CREDIT

SEC. 852. (a) A participant may, subject to the provisions of this section, include in his period of service—

(1) service performed as a civilian officer or employee of the Government prior to becoming a participant; and

(2) active military or naval service in the Army, Navy, Marine Corps, or Coast Guard of the United States.

(b) A person may obtain credit for prior service by making a special contribution to the Fund equal to 5 per centum of his annual salary for each year of service for which credit is sought subsequent to July 1, 1924, with interest thereon to date of payment compounded annually at 4 per centum. Any such participant may, under such conditions as may be determined in each instance by the Secretary, pay such special contributions in installments during the continuance of his service.

(c) Nothing in this Act shall be construed so as to affect in any manner a participant's right to retired pay, pension, or compensation in addition to the annuities herein provided, but no participant may obtain prior service credit toward an annuity under the Foreign Service Retirement and Disability System for any period of service, whether in a civilian or military capacity, on the basis of which he is receiving or will in the future be entitled to receive any annuity, pension, or other retirement or disability payment or allowance.

EXTRA SERVICE CREDIT FOR SERVICE AT UNHEALTHFUL POSTS

SEC. 853. The President may from time to time establish a list of places which by reason of climatic or other extreme conditions are to be classed as unhealthful posts, and each year of duty subsequent to January 1, 1900, at such posts inclusive of regular leaves of absence, of participants thereafter retired, shall be counted as one year and a half, and so on in like proportion in reckoning the length of service for the purpose of retirement, fractional months being considered as full months in computing such service. The President may at any time cancel the designation of any places as unhealthful without affecting any credit which has accrued for service at such posts prior to the date of the cancellation.

CREDIT FOR SERVICE WHILE ON MILITARY LEAVE

SEC. 854. Contributions shall not be required covering periods of leave of absence from the Service granted a participant while performing active military or naval service in the Army, Navy, Marine Corps, or Coast Guard of the United States.

Part G—Moneys

ESTIMATE OF APPROPRIATIONS NEEDED

Sec. 861. The Secretary of the Treasury shall prepare the estimates of the annual appropriations required to be made to the Fund, and shall make actuarial valuations of such funds at intervals of five years, or oftener if deemed necessary by him. The Secretary of State may expend from money to the credit of the Fund an amount not exceeding $5,000 per annum for the incidental expenses necessary in administering the provisions of this title, including actuarial advice.

ANNUAL REPORT TO CONGRESS

Sec. 862. The Secretary shall submit annually to the President and to the Congress a comparative report showing the condition of the Fund and estimates of appropriations necessary to continue this title in full force.

INVESTMENT OF MONEYS IN THE FUND

Sec. 863. The Secretary of the Treasury shall invest from time to time in interest-bearing securities of the United States such portions of the Fund as in his judgment may not be immediately required for the payment of annuities, cash benefits, refunds, and allowances, and the income derived from such investments shall constitute a part of such Fund.

ATTACHMENT OF MONEYS

Sec. 864. None of the moneys mentioned in this title shall be assignable either in law or equity, or be subject to execution, levy, attachment, garnishment, or other legal process, except as provided in section 634 (b).

Part H—Officers Reinstated in the Service

Sec. 871. A Foreign Service officer, reinstated in the Service in accordance with the provisions of section 520 (b) shall, while so serving, be entitled in lieu of his retirement allowance to the full pay of the class in which he is temporarily serving. During such service, he shall make contributions to the Fund in accordance with the provisions of section 811. If the annuity he was receiving prior to his reinstatement in the Service was based on less than thirty years of service credit, the amount of his annuity when he reverts to the retired list shall be recomputed on the basis of his total service credit.

PART I—VOLUNTARY CONTRIBUTIONS

SEC. 881. (a) Any participant may, at his option and under such regulations as may be prescribed by the President, deposit additional sums in multiples of 1 per centum of his basic salary, but not in excess of 10 per centum of such salary, which amounts together with interest at 3 per centum per annum, compounded on June 30 of each year shall, at the date of his retirement and at his election, be—

(1) returned to him in a lump sum; or

(2) used to purchase an additional life annuity; or

(3) used to purchase an additional life annuity for himself and to provide for a cash payment on his death to a beneficiary whose name shall be notified in writing to the Secretary by the participant; or

(4) used to purchase an additional life annuity for himself and a life annuity commencing on his death payable to a beneficiary whose name shall be notified in writing to the Secretary by the participant with a guaranteed return to the beneficiary or his legal representative of an amount equal to the cash payment referred to in paragraph 3.

(b) The benefits provided by subparagraphs 2, 3, or 4 of paragraph (a) of this section shall be actuarially equivalent in value to the payment provided for by paragraph (a) (1) of this section and shall be calculated upon such tables of mortality as may be from time to time prescribed for this purpose by the Secretary of the Treasury.

(c) In case a participant shall become separated from the Service for any reason except retirement on an annuity, the amount of any additional deposits with interest at 3 per centum per annum, compounded annually, made by him under the provisions of this paragraph shall be refunded in the manner provided in section 841 for the return of contributions and interest in the case of death or withdrawal from active service.

(d) Any benefits payable to an officer or to his beneficiary in respect to the additional deposits provided under this paragraph shall be in addition to the benefits otherwise provided under this title.

TITLE IX—ALLOWANCES AND BENEFITS

Part A—Allowances and Special Allotments

QUARTERS, COST OF LIVING, AND REPRESENTATION ALLOWANCES

Sec. 901. In accordance with such regulations as the President may prescribe and notwithstanding the provisions of section 1765 of the Revised Statutes (5 U. S. C. 70), the Secretary is authorized to grant to any officer or employee of the Service who is a citizen of the United States—

(1) allowances, wherever Government owned or rented quarters are not available, for living quarters, heat, light, fuel, gas, and electricity, including allowances for the cost of lodging at temporary quarters, incurred by an officer or employee of the Service and the members of his family upon first arrival at a new post, for a period not in excess of three months after such first arrival or until the occupation of residence quarters, whichever period shall be shorter, up to but not in excess of the aggregate amount of the per diem that would be allowable to such officer or employee for himself and the members of his family for such period if they were in travel status;

(2) cost-of-living allowances, whenever the Secretary shall determine—

(i) that the cost of living at a post abroad is proportionately so high that an allowance is necessary to enable an officer or employee of the Service at such post to carry on his work efficiently;

(ii) that extraordinary and necessary expenses, not otherwise compensated for, are incurred by an officer or employee of the Service incident to the establishment of his residence at his post of assignment;

(iii) that an allowance is necessary to assist an officer or employee of the Service who is compelled by reason of dangerous, notably unhealthful, or excessively adverse living conditions at his post abroad or for the convenience of the Government to meet the additional expense of maintaining his wife and minor children elsewhere than in the country of his assignment;

(3) allowances in order to provide for the proper representation of the United States by officers or employees of the Service.

ALLOTMENT FOR OFFICIAL RESIDENCE OF CHIEF AMERICAN REPRESENTATIVE

SEC. 902. The Secretary may, under such regulations as he may prescribe, make an allotment of funds to any post to defray the unusual expenses incident to the operation and maintenance of an official residence suitable for the chief representative of the United States at that post.

ACCOUNTING FOR ALLOWANCES

SEC. 903. All such allowances and allotments shall be accounted for to the Secretary in such manner and under such rules and regulations as the President may prescribe. The Secretary shall report all such expenditures annually to the Congress with the budget estimates of the Department.

PART B—TRAVEL AND RELATED EXPENSES

GENERAL PROVISIONS

SEC. 911. The Secretary may, under such regulations as he shall prescribe, pay—

(1) the travel expenses of officers and employees of the Service, including expenses incurred while traveling pursuant to orders issued by the Secretary in accordance with the provisions of section 933 with regard to the granting of home leave;

(2) the travel expenses of the members of the family of an officer or employee of the Service when proceeding to or return-

ing from his post of duty; accompanying him on authorized home leave; or otherwise traveling in accordance with authority granted pursuant to the terms of this or any other Act;

(3) the cost of transporting the furniture and household and personal effects of an officer or employee of the Service to his successive posts of duty and, on the termination of his services, to the place where he will reside;

(4) the cost of storing the furniture and household and personal effects of an officer or employee of the Service who is absent under orders from his usual post of duty, or who is assigned to a post to which, because of emergency conditions, he cannot take or at which he is unable to use, his furniture and household and personal effects;

(5) the cost of storing the furniture and household and personal effects of an officer or employee of the Service on first arrival at a post for a period not in excess of three months after such first arrival at such post or until the establishment of residence quarters, whichever shall be shorter;

(6) the travel expenses of the members of the family and the cost of transporting the personal effects and automobile of an officer or employee of the Service, whenever the travel of such officer or employee is occasioned by changes in the seat of the government whose capital is his post;

(7) the travel expenses and transportation costs incident to the removal of the members of the family of an officer or employee of the Service and his furniture and household and personal effects, including automobiles, from a post at which, because of the prevalence of disturbed conditions, there is imminent danger to life and property, and the return of such persons, furniture, and effects to such post upon the cessation of such conditions; or to such other post as may in the meantime have become the post to which such officer or employee has been assigned.

(8) the cost of preparing and transporting to their former homes in the continental United States or to a place not more distant, the remains of an officer or employee of the Service who is a citizen of the United States and of the members of his family who may die abroad or while in travel status.

LOAN OF HOUSEHOLD EQUIPMENT

SEC. 912. The Secretary may, if he shall find it in the interests of the Government to do so as a means of eliminating transportation costs, provide officers and employees of the Service with household equipment for use on a loan basis in personally owned or leased residences.

TRANSPORTATION OF AUTOMOBILES

SEC. 913. The Secretary may, notwithstanding the provisions of any other law, transport for or on behalf of an officer or employee of the Service, a privately owned automobile in any case where he shall determine that water, rail, or air transportation of the automobile is necessary or expedient for any part or of all the distance between points of origin and destination.

PART C—COMMISSARY SERVICE

SEC. 921. The Secretary may, under such regulations as he may prescribe, and pursuant to appropriations therefor, establish and maintain emergency commissary or mess services in such places abroad where, in his judgment, such services are necessary temporarily to insure the effective and efficient performance of the duties and responsibilities of the Service, such services to be available to the officers and employees of all Government agencies located in any such places abroad. Reimbursements incident to the maintenance and operation of commissary or mess service shall be at not less than cost as determined by the Secretary and shall be used as working funds: *Provided,* That each year an amount equal to the amount of the appropriation for such service shall be covered into the Treasury as miscellaneous receipts not later than six months after the close of the fiscal year for which any such appropriation is made.

PART D—LEAVES OF ABSENCE

ANNUAL LEAVE

SEC. 931. (a) The Secretary may, in his discretion and in accordance with such regulations as he may prescribe, grant an officer or employee of the Service who is a citizen of the United States not ₁₀ exceed sixty calendar days' annual leave of absence with pay.

(b) Where an officer or employee on leave returns to the continental United States, the leave of absence granted pursuant to the provisions of paragraph (a) of this section shall be exclusive of the time actually and necessarily occupied in going to and from the continental United States, and such time as may be necessarily occupied in awaiting sailing or flight.

(c) Any part of the sixty days' annual leave which an officer or employee may receive and which is not used in any one year shall be accumulated for succeeding years until it totals one hundred and eighty days.

(d) The Secretary may in his discretion and subject to such regulations as he may prescribe, grant to an employee of the Service who is not a citizen of the United States thirty calendar days' annual leave with pay each calendar year. Any part of the thirty days' leave not used in any year shall be accumulated for succeeding years until it totals not exceeding sixty days.

SICK LEAVE

SEC. 932. The Secretary may in his discretion and subject to such regulations as he may prescribe, grant an officer or employee of the Service sick leave with pay at the rate of fifteen calendar days each calendar year. Any part of the fifteen days' sick leave not used or availed of in any year shall be accumulated for succeeding years until it totals one hundred and twenty days.

ORDERING RETURN OF PERSONNEL TO UNITED STATES ON LEAVES OF ABSENCE

SEC. 933. (a) The Secretary shall order to the continental United States on statutory leave of absence every officer and employee of the Service who is a citizen of the United States upon completion of two years' continuous service abroad or as soon as possible thereafter.

(b) While in the continental United States on leave, the service of any officer or employee shall be available for such work or duties

[203]

in the Department or elsewhere as the Secretary may prescribe, but the time of such work or duties shall not be counted as leave.

RESERVE OFFICERS ASSIGNED TO THE SERVICE

SEC. 934. (a) A Reserve officer, assigned to the Service from any Government agency shall, notwithstanding the provisions of any other law, be granted annual leave of absence and sick leave of absence in accordance with the provisions of part D of this title during the period of his assignment.

(b) Under such regulations as the President may prescribe, a person assigned to the Service as a Reserve officer from any Government agency may, notwithstanding the provisions of the Act of December 21, 1944 (58 Stat. 845; 5 U. S. C. 61b), transfer to the Service any annual or sick leave of absence standing to his credit at the time of his assignment to the Service. On his return to the agency by which he is regularly employed, he may transfer the aggregate of his accumulated and current annual and sick leave to that agency but the amount of leave so transferred shall not exceed the maximum which an officer or employee of the agency to which he is returning may have to his credit on the date of his return.

TRANSFER OF LEAVE OF ABSENCE

SEC. 935. Under such regulations as the President may prescribe an officer or employee of the Service who resigns from the Service in order to accept an appointment in any Government agency may transfer to such Government agency any annual or sick leave of absence standing to his credit at the time of his resignation from the Service and any officer or employee of any Government agency who resigns from such agency in order to accept an appointment to the Service may transfer to the Service any annual or sick leave of absence standing to his credit at the time of his resignation from the Government agency in which he was employed, but in no event shall the amount of annual or sick leave of absence so transferred exceed the maximum amount of the annual or sick leave of absence which may be accumulated in either the Service or the Government agency to which such person is appointed, as the case may be.

Part E—Medical Services

EXPENSES OF TREATMENT

Sec. 941. The Secretary may, in the event of illness or injury requiring hospitalization of an officer or employee of the Service who is a citizen of the United States, not the result of vicious habits, intemperance, or misconduct on his part, incurred in the line of duty while such person is assigned abroad, pay for the cost of the treatment of such illness or injury at a suitable hospital or clinic.

TRANSPORTATION TO APPROVED HOSPITALS

Sec. 942. (a) The Secretary may, in the event of illness or injury requiring the hospitalization of an officer or employee of the Service who is a citizen of the United States, not the result of vicious habits, intemperance, or misconduct on his part, incurred while on assignment abroad, in a locality where there does not exist a suitable hospital or clinic, pay the travel expenses of such officer or employee by whatever means he shall deem appropriate and without regard to the Standardized Government Travel Regulations and section 10 of the Act of March 3, 1933 (47 Stat. 1516; 5 U. S. C. 73b), to the nearest locality where a suitable hospital or clinic exists and on his recovery pay for the travel expenses of his return to his post of duty. If the officer or employee is too ill to travel unattended, the Secretary may also pay the travel expenses of an attendant.

(b) The Secretary may establish a first-aid station and provide for the services of a nurse at a post at which, in his opinion, sufficient personnel is employed to warrant such a station.

PHYSICAL EXAMINATIONS AND COSTS OF INOCULATIONS

Sec. 943. The Secretary shall, under such regulations as he may prescribe, provide for the periodic physical examination of officers and employees of the Service who are citizens of the United States, including examinations necessary to establish disability or incapacity in accordance with the provisions of section 831, and for the cost of administering inoculations or vaccinations to such officers or employees.

TITLE X—MISCELLANEOUS

PART A—PROHIBITIONS

AGAINST UNIFORMS

SEC. 1001. An officer or employee of the Service holding a position of responsibility in the Service shall not wear any uniform except such as may be authorized by law or such as a military commander may require civilians to wear in a theater of military operations.

AGAINST ACCEPTING PRESENTS

SEC. 1002. An officer or employee of the Service shall not ask or, without the consent of the Congress, receive, for himself or any other person, any present, emolument, pecuniary favor, office, or title from any foreign government. A chief of mission or other principal officer may, however, under such regulations as the President may prescribe, accept gifts made to the United States or to any political subdivision thereof by the government to which he is accredited or from which he holds an exequatur.

AGAINST ENGAGING IN BUSINESS ABROAD

SEC. 1003. An officer or employee of the Service shall not, while holding office, transact or be interested in any business or engage for profit in any profession in the country or countries to which he is assigned abroad in his own name or in the name or through the agency of any other person, except as authorized by the Secretary.

AGAINST CORRESPONDENCE ON AFFAIRS OF FOREIGN GOVERNMENTS

SEC. 1004. (a) An officer or employee of the Service shall not correspond in regard to the public affairs of any foreign government except with the proper officers of the United States, except as authorized by the Secretary.

(b) An officer or employee of the Service shall not recommend any person for employment in any position of trust or profit under the government of the country to which he is detailed or assigned, except as authorized by the Secretary.

AGAINST POLITICAL, RACIAL, RELIGIOUS, OR COLOR DISCRIMINATION

SEC. 1005. In carrying out the provisions of this Act, no political test shall be required and none shall be taken into consideration, nor shall there be any discrimination against any person on account of race, creed, or color.

PART B—BONDS

SEC. 1011. Every secretary, consul general, consul, vice consul, Foreign Service officer, and Foreign Service Reserve officer, and, if required, any other officer or employee of the Service or of the Department before he enters upon the duties of his office shall give to the United States a bond in such form and in such penal sum as the Secretary shall prescribe, with such sureties as the Secretary shall approve, conditioned without division of penalty for the true and faithful performance of his duties, including (but not by way of limitation) certifying vouchers for payment, accounting for, paying over, and delivering up of all fees, moneys, goods, effects, books, records, papers, and other property that shall come to his hands or to the hands of any other person to his use as such officer or employee under any law now or hereafter enacted and for the true and faithful performance of all other duties now or hereafter lawfully imposed upon him as such officer or employee, and such bond shall be construed to be conditioned for the true and faithful performance of all official duties of whatever character now or hereafter lawfully imposed upon him, or by him assumed incident to his employment as an officer or employee of the Government. Notwithstanding any other provisions of law, upon approval of any bond given pursuant to this Act, the principal shall not be required to give another separate bond conditioned for the true and faithful performance of only a part of the duties for which the bond given pursuant to this Act is conditioned. The bond of an officer or employee of the Service shall be construed to be conditioned for the true and faithful performance of all acts of such officer incident to his office regardless of whether appointed or commissioned as diplomatic, consular, Foreign Service officer, or other officer of the Service. The bonds herein mentioned shall be deposited with the Secretary of the Treasury. Nothing herein con-

[207]

tained shall be deemed to obviate the necessity of furnishing any bond which may be required pursuant to the provisions of the Subsistence Expense Act of 1926, as amended (44 Stat. 688; 47 Stat. 405; 56 Stat. 39; 5 U. S. C. 821-823, 827-833) .

PART C—GIFTS

SEC. 1021. (a) The Secretary may accept on behalf of the United States gifts made unconditionally by will or otherwise for the benefit of the Service or for the carrying out of any of its functions. Conditional gifts may be so accepted if recommended by the Director General, and the principal of and income from any such conditional gift shall be held, invested, reinvested, and used in accordance with its conditions, but no gift shall be accepted which is conditioned upon any expenditure not to be met therefrom or from the income thereof unless such expenditure has been approved by Act of Congress.

(b) Any unconditional gift of money accepted pursuant to the authority granted in paragraph (a) of this section, the net proceeds from the liquidation (pursuant to paragraph (c) or paragraph (d) of this section) of any other property so accepted, and the proceeds of insurance on any such gift property not used for its restoration, shall be deposited in the Treasury of the United States and are hereby appropriated and shall be held in trust by the Secretary of the Treasury for the benefit of the Service, and he may invest and reinvest such funds in interest-bearing obligations of the United States or in obligations guaranteed as to both principal and interest by the United States. Such gifts and the income from such investments shall be available for expenditure in the operation of the Service and the performance of its functions, subject to the same examination and audit as is provided for appropriations made for the Service by Congress.

(c) The evidences of any unconditional gift of intangible personal property, other than money, accepted pursuant to the authority granted in paragraph (a) of this section, shall be deposited with the Secretary of the Treasury and he, in his discretion, may hold them, or liquidate them except that they shall be liquidated upon the request of the Secretary whenever necessary to meet payments required in the operation of the Service or the performance of its functions. The proceeds and income from any such property held by the Secretary of the Treasury shall be available for expenditure as is provided in paragraph (b) of this section.

(d) The Secretary shall hold any real property or any tangible personal property accepted unconditionally pursuant to the authority granted in paragraph (a) of this section and he shall permit such property to be used for the operation of the Service and the performance of its functions or he may lease or hire such property, and may insure such property, and deposit the income thereof with the Secretary of the Treasury to be available for expenditure as provided in paragraph (b) of this section. The income from any such real property or tangible personal property shall be available for expenditure in the discretion of the Secretary for the maintenance, preservation, or repair and insurance of such property and any proceeds from insurance may be used to restore the property insured. Any such property when not required for the operation of the Service or the performance of its functions may be liquidated by the Secretary, and the proceeds thereof deposited with the Secretary of the Treasury, whenever in his judgment the purposes of the gifts will be served thereby.

(e) For the purpose of Federal income, estate, and gift taxes, any gift, devise, or bequest accepted by the Secretary under authority of this Act shall be deemed to be a gift, devise, or bequest to or for the use of the United States.

Part D—Authorization to Retain Attorneys

Sec. 1031. The Secretary may, without regard to sections 189 and 365 of the Revised Statutes (5 U. S. C. 49 and 314), authorize a principal officer to procure legal services whenever such services are required for the protection of the interests of the Government or to enable an officer or employee of the Service to carry on his work efficiently.

Part E—Delegation of Authority

Sec. 1041. (a) The Secretary may delegate to officers or employees holding positions of responsibility in the Department or the Service or to such boards as he may continue or establish any of the powers conferred upon him by this Act to the extent that he finds such delegation to be in the interests of the efficient administration of the Service.

(b) The Director General may delegate to officers or employees holding positions of responsibility in the Department or the Service any of the powers conferred upon him by this Act to the extent that he finds such delegation to be in the interests of the efficient administration of the Service.

PART F—EXEMPTION FROM TAXATION

SEC. 1051. Section 116 of the Internal Revenue Code, as amended (53 Stat. 48; 53 Stat. 575; 56 Stat. 842; 58 Stat. 46; 26 U. S C. 116), relative to exclusions from gross income, is further amended by adding at the end thereof a new subsection to read as follows:

" (k) In the case of an officer or employee of the Foreign Service of the United States, amounts received by such officer or employee as allowances or otherwise under the terms of title IX of the Foreign Service Act of 1946."

PART G—INTERPRETATION OF THE ACT

LIBERAL-CONSTRUCTION CLAUSE

SEC. 1061. The provisions of this Act shall be construed liberally in order to effectuate its purpose.

PROVISIONS THAT MAY BE HELD INVALID

SEC. 1062. If any provision of this Act or the application of any such provision to any person or circumstance shall be held invalid, the validity of the remainder of the Act and the applicability of such provision to other persons or circumstances shall not be affected thereby.

HEADINGS OF TITLES, PARTS, AND SECTIONS

SEC. 1063. The headings descriptive of the various titles, parts, and sections of this Act are inserted for convenience only, and, in case of any conflict between any such heading and the substance of the title, part, or section to which it relates, the heading shall be disregarded.

PROVISIONS OF THE ACT OF JULY 3, 1946

SEC. 1064. Nothing in this Act shall be construed to affect the provisions of sections 1, 2, 3, and 4 of the Act of July 3, 1946 (Public Law 488, Seventy-ninth Congress). The "classified grades" within the meaning of that Act shall, from and after the effective date of this Act, be construed to mean classes 1 to 5, inclusive.

PART H—AUTHORIZATION FOR APPROPRIATIONS

SEC. 1071. Appropriations to carry out the purposes of this Act are hereby authorized.

APPENDIX B

THE BRITISH AND FRENCH
FOREIGN SERVICES

THE BRITISH and French Foreign Services are among the oldest career diplomatic and consular services maintained by the present world powers. They have a long and proud tradition behind them. Their present functioning represents experiences gained by a great number of brilliant officers who have exercised the talents of diplomacy on behalf of their respective countries over a period of centuries.

In their modern form the British and French diplomatic services date only from the beginning of the Sixteenth Century.* It was Cardinal Wolsey, the great Minister of Henry VIII, who was the architect of the modern British diplomatic service; the French service took shape under the personal direction of François I (1515-1547). It was about this time or a little earlier that most European monarchies established a special branch of administration for foreign affairs. However, it was 1589 before France had

---

* One of the most interesting accounts of the development of modern European diplomacy is to be found in an article contributed by E. Nys, *Les Commencements de la Diplomatie et le Droit d'Ambassade jusqu'à Grotius, Revue de Droit International,* LXVI, 1884. Cf. also J. Zeller, *La Diplomatie Française,* Hachette, Paris, 1881; Louis-Paul Deschanel, *Histoire de la Politique Extérieure de la France,* Payot, Paris, 1936; and L. de Gerin-Ricard, *Traditions de la Diplomatie Française,* Laffont, Paris, 1941.

a single Secretary of State, charged with the functions of a Minister for Foreign Affairs. Previous to that time such work had been shared by three French ministers. It was not until 1787 that the functions of such a single Secretary of State were confined exclusively to those of foreign affairs. In Great Britain the King's Secretary is first heard of in 1253, but in this case also his work was not confined to foreign affairs. Later there were even two Secretaries for Foreign Affairs, who divided between them the foreign affairs of the King according to geographical lines. Since 1782 the Secretaryship for Foreign Affairs has been entrusted in England to a single minister.

Under François I, most French envoys were men of the Church, ambassadors usually being recruited from among the ranks of bishops. Wolsey chose his permanent ambassadors generally from the lower classes, fearing to employ members of powerful families. The pay, whether in the British or French service, was meager. A British Ambassador usually received five shillings a day, exclusive of his allowances. Sometimes twenty shillings a day was paid him, but in that case he had to meet his own traveling expenses and those of his suite. The consequence was that most ambassadors supplemented their pay by subsidies, or bribes, received from the courts to which they were accredited. Wolsey himself was not above this practice; according to Nys, he received some £14,800 annually from François I. Writing of the corruption which reigned at the Sublime Porte, a Venetian Ambassador there reported in 1587 that "money was like wine which doctors prescribe equally to the well and sick."

Both the British and the French diplomatic services had a slow but progressive growth. Probably no country in the whole world was so well served by its diplomatic officers as was France in the period between its defeat by Germany in 1870 and the end of the First World War. France had suffered a disastrous reverse; yet, in the brief period of a generation, French diplomats, by their unadvertised and inconspicuous work, established the diplomatic supremacy of France in the councils of Europe to a degree which was the envy of its late victorious adversary, Germany.

These two senior foreign services by their well-earned prestige and by the traditions they have established, have exerted great influence in the development of other foreign services, including our own.

THE BRITISH FOREIGN SERVICE

THE PRESENT ORGANIZATION of the British Foreign Service came into being in 1943 with the amalgamation of the Foreign Office and Diplomatic Service, the Consular Service, and the Commercial Diplomatic Service into one self-contained and separate Service of the Crown.

The minister responsible to Parliament for British foreign relations and for the operations of the Foreign Service is the Secretary of State for Foreign Affairs. He is supported by two ministers; the Minister of State and the Parliamentary Under Secretary who supervise certain aspects of the work of the Foreign Office and assist him in answering in the House of Commons questions on foreign affairs. The Minister of State is served by a professional staff of career officers both in the Foreign Office and at diplomatic missions and consular posts abroad. When the organization of the British Foreign Service has been completed on the basis of the reforms of 1943 this staff will be composed of five branches, the members of which will be interchangeable between the Foreign Office and posts abroad.

The senior of these branches is known as Branch A. This branch provides the ambassadors, ministers, counselors, and secretaries at diplomatic missions; the consuls general, consuls and vice-consuls at consular posts; and the higher officials such as under secretaries, the legal advisers, and the bulk of the staff of the political departments in the Foreign Office.

Branch B will consist of officers who now belong to the executive and clerical grades of the home service and will staff a number of technical posts in the Foreign Office and posts such as those of accountant, archivist, code officer, and clerk in the Foreign Office and abroad. It is also intended to make a member of Branch A posts available to suitably qualified members of Branch B and to provide openings for promotions from Branch B to Branch A.

Branch C will consist of typists; Branch D of King's Foreign Service Messengers (couriers) ; and Branch E of subordinate staff such as building superintendents, chancery servants, and messengers.

In 1939 the three services amalgamated in Branch A of the British Foreign Service contained some 600 officers, of whom about 130 served in diplomatic posts, 350 in consular, 50 in commercial diplomatic, and only about 70 in the Foreign Office. There were in addition some 500 consular officials in a lower category of rank and about 1,300 in the executive and clerical grades at home and abroad, of whom rather more than half were permanent civil servants. On April 1, 1940 the American Foreign Service comprised 851 officers, of whom 707 were in diplomatic or consular posts, 51 in commercial diplomatic posts, 70 in the Department of State, 7 on special and temporary detail, and 16 in the Foreign Service Officers' Training School.

The permanent head of the British Foreign Service and of the Foreign Office and the principal adviser of the Secretary of State is the Permanent Under Secretary of State. He is a member of the Foreign Service and provides that continuity of policy through different changes of government so essential to a coherent foreign policy. There is no comparable official in the United States Department of State at present: In the British Service the Permanent Under Secretary is assisted by a number of other Under Secretaries, likewise career officers, who supervise the work of the various divisions (called Departments) of the Foreign Office. There are thirty-three Departments and most of them are headed by counselors.

The distribution of the work among these thirty-three Departments corresponds in general to the distribution of work in the Department of State among the different divisions. In the British Foreign Office the Departments fall within three main groups: (1) technical Departments, which organize and administer the Service; (2) political Departments, each of whose functions concern a special country or group of countries. (Because of this they are known as the "geographical" Departments) ; and (3) those Departments whose functions although political in the sense that they, too, deal with questions concerning British relations with foreign countries, concern themselves primarily with subjects or group of subjects, rather than with areas of earth.

The technical Departments comprise what are known as the Establishment: Finance, Personnel, Archives, Communications, Treaty, Passport and Passport Control (visa) Departments, and the Library. The "subject" Departments are the Consular, Cultural Relations, Dominions Intelligence, Economic Intelligence, Economic Relations, Economic Warfare, Economic and Industrial Planning, General, News, Prisoners of War, Reconstruction, Refugees, Services Liaison, and Supply and Relief.

The "geographical" Departments, corresponding to the four "geographic" Offices of the Department of State * are the Eastern, Egyptian, Far Eastern, German, Northern, North American, South American, Southern and Western Departments.

As in the case of the four corresponding Offices of the Department of State the "geographical" Departments of the British Foreign Office deal with a great variety of problems arising in or in connection with the foreign countries which they cover. Together with the "subject" Departments they constitute the political intelligence and advisory bureau which collects and analyzes information about events and developments in foreign countries, received from Foreign Service officers abroad and from other sources, with the object of assisting the Secretary of State in the formulation of policy. They have also the tasks of keeping other departments of the British Government informed of matters abroad which interest them; of preparing, in agreement with these other departments where necessary, instructions and guidance for members of the Service, who represent, not only the Foreign Office, but the whole of the British Government abroad; of negotiating with and making representations to the representatives of foreign governments in London, and dealing with their inquiries and representations; and of giving advice and help to firms and individuals in Great Britain who have interests abroad. It will be observed that the outline of the functions of those Departments corresponds precisely, *mutatis mutandis,* with the functions of the geographic Offices of the Department of State, namely the Offices of Far Eastern, American Republics, European, and Near Eastern and African Affairs.

* Cf. Chapter III, page 36 ff.

FOREIGN OFFICE PROCEDURE

It is perhaps in the minutiae of British Foreign Office procedure rather than in organization that the greatest difference lies between it and the Department of State.

A letter, official despatch, or other written document received at the Foreign Office passes first to the Classification or Opening Branch and is there placed in a white paper folder known as a "jacket." The document is held in the jacket by a tag on which sheets of paper containing minutes or drafts can be threaded without fear of loss or confusion. This jacket is stamped with the letter or letters indicating the department within whose sphere the subject comes. The jacket is then sent to the Division of Registry of that Department where it is entered. "Entering" consists of giving the jacket a file number concerned with the subject in question, indexing it, and attaching a brief summary of the contents to the outside of the jacket. When entered, the document in its jacket is known as a *paper*. A copy of the summary, with the number of the paper, is kept in the Division on a dummy jacket on which movements of the live jacket are marked, so that the latter can be located, wherever it may be, when required. This is important since many papers concern more than one Department and would be lost unless track was kept of them in the Division. It is essential to the working of the system that Departments should return papers to the Division when they have taken action on them. After action has been finally taken on the papers they go for permanent indexing and filing to the Main Index Section of the Archives Department.

Under the procedure used in the Department of State, papers are jacketed, given a file number and subject heading, entered in the records, and endorsed with the symbols of those Offices and Divisions of the Department to which they are to be routed, the initial one being that responsible for the taking of action. A procedure is adhered to, as in the British Foreign Office, for keeping track of papers as they circulate. However, the procedure for indexing in the Department of State is entirely centralized in one single Division instead of being distributed among different Divisions. The British decentralization is believed to offer many advantages, as it places the initial responsibility for properly identifying the paper with the Divisions which are thoroughly familiar with the subject. The British procedure would eliminate the incredible confusion which arose in the identification of papers at the beginning of the war. Most of the papers received in the Department of State were classified "European War" with the result that it became almost impossible to recover a paper once it had passed to the files. The indexing system of the State Department is believed to require drastic overhauling and attention might well be given to its possible decentralization.

Four types of jacket are used in the British Foreign Office. Ordinary correspondence is placed in a white jacket on which the markings and numbers are in black; telegrams go into a similar jacket on which the markings are in red; highly confidential or secret papers go into a jacket which bears a broad green band across the top; while pink or blue jackets are reserved for most secret *papers* which must not be compromised. *Papers* in this last category are retained by the Department concerned and do not pass through the hands of the registry Divisions. Moreover, no action may be taken on such *papers* without the prior concurrence of the private secretary to the Permanent Under Secretary.

The entered *paper* is sent with any earlier *papers* on the subject to the Department for action where, in normal and not urgent cases, it is passed to the junior official, corresponding to the "desk" or country officer in the Department of State, who deals with the subject in question. The business of that official is to study the *paper* and in the light of anything that may have passed before on the matter, to decide what action is needed. He then writes a *minute* on the outside of the jacket, signs it and passes the *paper* to his superior. The purpose of the *minute* is to indicate what action is called for on the *paper* in question. It may be that all that is needed is to mark on the jacket a direction that a copy of the communication in it is to be sent to another government department to which it is of interest. Some *papers* require no action and are sent merely for the information of the Foreign Office. Many of them need no *minutes*—especially from junior officers;

such papers are merely signed and passed on. On other *papers*, junior officers are expected to draw the attention of their superiors to certain passages in a despatch or considerations arising from it.

A former Librarian of the British Foreign Office has written:

"It is but seldom that an official of our own or any other Foreign Office can, on the receipt of a despatch, note, telegram, or private letter, sit down and attempt to dictate, or make a draft for, a reply without the consultation of any of his colleagues, inside or outside the Office. In nine cases out of ten he will wish to obtain the advice of his equals and the approval of his superiors before taking any decisive action: and such advice and approval he solicits ordinarily by means of *minutes,* and occasionally through exploratory memoranda.

"The *minutes* assume that the next person or persons to whom the paper is submitted will have time to read its contents and to examine sufficiently the previous papers containing the substance of the question at issue. The *minute* writer calls attention to the essence of any topic newly raised or any new aspect of a matter already the subject of correspondence and proposes the action he considers desirable upon it: whether an immediate reply can be given, or whether it should be referred to other authorities, inside or outside the Office, for advice before final action. He confines his proposals to the briefest possible terms; compression is only next valuable to clarity in the conduct of this part of official business."

One of the functions of the junior officer examining the jacket is to make sure that the *paper* being considered is properly routed to all those Departments of the Foreign Office which may be interested in it. Junior officers are expected to sign their *minutes* in full; the officer authorizing action or deciding that no action is needed and that no one higher up than he need see the *paper,* "initials it off." When finished with, the *paper* is returned to the registry Division.

If an outgoing letter, despatch * or telegram is called for, a draft is prepared on special blue-gray paper to avoid any possible confusion of the draft with the *minute* on which it is based. When the draft has been seen by all concerned and given the final initial

* The British employ "despatch" to indicate formal written communications exchanged between the Foreign Office and its representatives abroad. In American practice such communications originating from the Department of State are termed "instructions," while those originating in the field are known as "despatches."

of the officer approving it, it is sent to the registry Division for copying, indexing, and transmission.

All this may seem very minute, but it is the very essence of a smooth functioning Foreign Office or Department of State. Our own procedure, while similar generally in practice, is by no means so well laid down and defined as to result in a single well-recognized system with which everyone is expected to conform.

The jackets of *papers* in the Department of State are indistinguishable, whether the subject is nonconfidential, confidential, secret, or top secret. The new *paper* is briefed by a junior officer as in the British Foreign Office, with a recommendation concerning the action, if any, to be taken. Such an officer is also responsible for seeing that copies of the paper go to other interested government departments and routing it to other possibly interested Divisions in the Department of State. There is no well defined system of *minuting*, however. In certain Offices or Divisions of the Department most of the work may be done through memorandums, corresponding to the British *minutes,* while in others it may be done verbally, through conference. The great advantage of the British system is that a permanent record is preserved so that any officer may at any time consult a jacket and have at a glance a written record of the case. In too many cases in the Department of State, the record is lost as memory of the details fades from an officer's mind.

The British system has so much to commend it that the Department of State might well undertake a thorough study to determine to what extent and with what changes it might be adapted to the Department of State. The British Foreign Office is an old and highly successful institution and the art of diplomacy, which consists so largely of written instruments, is one to the practice of which we have come late. There is much, it is believed, that we might adopt advantageously from the procedure of the British Foreign Office, particularly in the mere mechanics of handling and disposing of papers.

BRITISH EXAMINATIONS FOR THE FOREIGN SERVICE

Candidates for the Branch A of the British Foreign Service, which is so far restricted to men, must have attained the age of 21 and must not be over 30 on the first day of August in which the examination is held. They must be natural-born British subjects and have been born within the United Kingdom or within one of the self-governing Dominions of parents who both answer the same qualifications, except that, when the circumstances are such as to justify departure from these requirements, a candidate may be allowed to compete by special permission of the Secretary of State for Foreign Affairs, provided that he fulfills the conditions in respect of nationality prescribed for candidates for admission to British Civil Establishments in general.

Every candidate must have obtained a degree with at least second-class honors at an institution of university rank, or have had whole-time, continuous, and systematic education until at least the age of 18, or satisfy the Civil Service Commissioners that he has received equivalent instruction which makes him fit for appointment.

Candidates are required to produce evidence of their ability to learn foreign languages, and to satisfy the Commissioners as to their health and character.

Candidates must fill in an appropriate application form obtainable from the Civil Service Commission. A fee of £1 is required to accompany the completed form. Those candidates who, from their application forms and the resulting inquiries, are found to be *prima facie* eligible are then required to undergo a qualifying written examination, consisting of tests in English, arithmetic, general culture, and general intelligence.

Candidates, who reach the qualifying standard in the written examination and satisfy the Commissioners of their linguistic ability, are thereafter subject to tests of personal qualities. Formerly these tests were conducted by an interviewing board but in 1945 resort was had to a "residential" method of testing which had been previously employed by the British Army and Navy. Candidates were assembled, after payment of a fee of £3, at the Manor House, Stoke d'Abernon, in Surrey. Here in the quiet of the English countryside they spent several days under constant observation, both individually and in groups, by trained observers. During their stay they were put through a series of carefully devised and harmonized tests. At the end their personality and fitness for appointments as British Foreign Service officers were assessed in a balanced judgment toward which each member of the team of observers contributed his considered opinion. The team, on the occasion of the first trial of the system, consisted of representatives of the Civil Service Commissioners and the Foreign Office, as well as three psychologists.

The argument in favor of such a procedure is that three days' observation of a candidate under residential conditions is likely to afford the government a better idea of a candidate's fitness than a half-hour interview, in which he can be judged only as an individual, and not as member of a group.

The aims of the Civil Service Selection Board, by which name the team which tests the candidates residentially is known, are:

1) To obtain as clear and accurate a picture as possible of the candidate's whole personality and, in particular, of his ability in those fields of activity for which he is being examined, taking into account his previous training and experience.

2) By a study of the candidate's character and temperament, and of the influences that have helped to mould them, and by taking into account his successes or failures in the past (in fact his whole past history) to attempt to forecast how he is likely to develop in the future.

The board attempts this task through practical tests, the basic principle of which is to observe the candidate at work on a wide range of problems of the same fundamental nature as those he may encounter later. Such tests comprise the following subjects:

a) Policy questions. Recognizing the existence of a problem, suggesting the solution, and advising generally on questions of policy.

b) Critical analysis in writing, including the analysis of reports, facts, or figures; and the production of an accurate summary or conclusions.

c) Persuasive exposition in writing, covering the writing of clear and acceptable *minutes,* reports, and letters.

d) Organizing ability, such as staff management and the ability to delegate when necessary.

e) Committee work, including oral exposition of complex subjects and the ability to carry some weight in any discussions.

[222]

f) Negotiation, either inside the Service or with outside organizations, including organizations in foreign countries.

g) Personal relations, long-term, including those with colleagues.

h) Personal relations, first contact. This covers a wider range of short-term contacts with outside officials, members of the general public, and general social relations.

i) Judgment of character.

j) Reaction to isolation. Self-control and self-sufficiency in lonely, dull, or remote posts.

k) Behavior in a crisis. The ability to act with firmness, decision, and resource in an isolated post in moments of political or social crisis.

l) Public speaking, not to be regarded as essential but as a definite asset.

m) Linguistic facility.

The recommendations of the board are submitted to the Civil Service Commissioners, for the information and use of the Final Selection Board whose task it is to place the candidates in a final order of merit based on their written and residential tests. Any attempt on the part of a candidate to enlist support for his application through Members of Parliament or other influential persons, except as references named by him in the application form, disqualifies him for appointment.

CONDITIONS OF SERVICE

Successful candidates for the British Foreign Service enter in the grade equivalent to that of third secretary or vice-consul at an annual salary of £275 ($1,100) rising by annual increases of £25 or £30 ($100 to $120) to £625 ($2,500). A British first secretary or consul has a salary ranging from $3,200 to $4,400, while a counselor or consul general receives from $4,600 to $6,000. (See Appendix A for comparison with United States Foreign Service salaries.)

Above the grades of counselor and consul general, a British Foreign Service officer may aspire to the posts of Assistant Under Secretary of State, Deputy Under Secretary of State, and Permanent Under Secretary of State in the Foreign Office, and minister and ambassador abroad, with salaries rising as high as £3,000 ($12,000). In addition to their salaries, British Foreign Service officers receive very substantial allowances of various kinds.

FUNCTIONS OF BRITISH FOREIGN SERVICE OFFICERS

The functions of the British Foreign Service officer as defined by the British Government are, *mutatis mutandis,* similar to those of the American Foreign Service officer. The British have set them forth as follows:

a) Members of the combined Foreign Service will have to serve at home in the Foreign Office or abroad in diplomatic, commercial diplomatic, or consular posts as the public service requires. They must have understanding of and interest in economic and commercial matters, and in social and labor problems, as well as in political questions. The function of the Foreign Service is, broadly, to represent His Majesty's Government in foreign countries and to be their channel of communication with foreign governments; to promote good relations with foreign countries; to protect British interests and to foster British trade. The art of diplomacy consists of making the policy of one government understood and, if possible, accepted by other governments.

b) Briefly and generally speaking, the work of a member of the Foreign Service in a diplomatic post consists of obtaining and supplying information about the foreign country where he is stationed and submitting advice thereon, in order that His Majesty's Government may be able to frame their policy towards that country; in negotiating with foreign officials on behalf of His Majesty's Government; and in representing this country. A Foreign Service officer abroad must therefore keep himself widely informed of what is going on in the country where he resides and learn to assess the importance of events and trends. He must be able to mix freely in all circles and to speak with knowledge of what his own country is and does.

c) In a commercial diplomatic post the work will involve studying and reporting on commercial and economic developments in the foreign country concerned, assisting British trade and reporting on commercial opportunities for British firms.

d) In a consular post, in addition to commercial reporting and to answering business inquiries and assisting British trade, a Foreign Service officer will have to protect British interests generally and fulfill various duties in connection with the Merchant Shipping Acts, registration of British subjects, passports and visas, repatriation of British subjects, perform notarial acts, etc. The Foreign Service officer abroad will have to play an active part in the affairs of the local British community who will frequently look to him for a lead. Much of the work at all posts abroad will consist of office work but the representational side is often more important and a Foreign Service officer must go about and get to know and be known by wide circles.

e) In the Foreign Office the work consists, broadly, of analyzing reports received from or about foreign countries with the objects of keeping other government departments informed and of giving the Foreign Secretary advice in the formulation of his policy, and of conveying, in harmony with the views of other government departments interested, the wishes and instructions of His Majesty's Government to their representatives abroad. For the performance of this work a man must be a good teamworker and possess good judgment, patience, ability to think and write clearly, as well as the ability to get on with his fellow men which is essential if foreigners are to be brought to accept or at least to understand this country's policy and point of view.

THE FRENCH FOREIGN SERVICE

THE ORGANIZATION of the French Foreign Service parallels in some respects that of the British Foreign Office and in others the American Department of State. Both the British Foreign Office and the American State Department have their counterpart, of course, in the French Ministry of Foreign Affairs, known to the public as the Quai d'Orsay by reason of its location, and referred to familiarly by its personnel as *"la maison."* The head of the Quai d'Orsay, who is responsible for the conduct of French foreign affairs, is the Minister for Foreign Affairs. He is a member of the French Cabinet.

Apart from the Minister for Foreign Affairs, the French Ministry of Foreign Affairs is staffed generally in its highest executive posts, as is the British Foreign Office, but unlike the Department of State, by senior members of the career French Foreign Service. As of November 1946, in the Department of State not only the Secretary of State but the Under Secretaries and four of the five Assistant Secretaries holding office have been appointed from public life and are subject to replacement with each change of administration.

The official in the French Foreign Ministry who corresponds to the Under Secretary of State in the Department of State and to Permanent Under Secretary of State in the British Foreign Office is known as the Secretary General. This post is usually held by a senior ambassador thoroughly acquainted with foreign affairs and with the organization both of the Ministry at home and the Foreign Service abroad. The choice of Secretary General may be but is not necessarily subject to the personal desires of the Minister for Foreign Affairs. The former, by his fixed tenure of office, provides that continuity of policy in both the technical and executive functions of Foreign Office work which makes for a co-ordinated foreign policy.

It has been seen that the work of the British Foreign Office is distributed among thirty-three different "Departments." This corresponds largely with the former organization of work in the Department of State among approximately the same number of Divisions. During the war, however, a new organizational structure was set up in the State Department and the Divisions which had expanded by that time to a number of some fifty-eight were grouped under and made responsible to twelve Offices headed by Directors. Such a structure corresponds more closely to the organization of the French Foreign Ministry.

The French Foreign Ministry is organized into eight principal offices, some but not all of which correspond to the twelve Offices of the Department of State. The forty odd sub-sections or divisions into which these are divided correspond more closely to the thirty-three Departments of the British Foreign Office and to the fifty odd Divisions of the Department of State than to the higher echelons.

The eight offices of the Foreign Ministry comprise those of: (1) political affairs; (2) economic, financial, and technical affairs; (3) administrative affairs; (4) cultural relations; (5) personnel, accounting, and supplies; (6) protocol; (7) codes; and (8) archives. The first four are headed by Directors General corresponding to Assistant Secretaries in the Department of State and to Under Secretaries in the British Foreign Office; the fifth is headed by a Director; and the last three by Chiefs of Service. Of the eight only one is in charge of a non-civil servant. This is the cultural relations section which is headed (in 1946) by a professor of the Faculty of Science in Paris. Officers of the French Foreign Service with the grade of minister plenipotentiary are in charge of the administrative and protocol sections, while consuls general are in charge of the offices having to do with personnel, codes, and archives. The two most important offices, those having to do with political and economic affairs, which are normally held by ambassadors or ministers of the career French Foreign Service, were in 1946 in charge of two inspectors of finance who played prominent roles in the French resistance movement. The holding of these key posts in the French Ministry of Foreign Affairs by officers who began their careers in the French civil service in the Ministry of Finance rather than in the Ministry of Foreign Affairs, reflected the importance attached by the French Government to questions of finance and economy in postwar international relations.

In view of their importance it may be useful to define in some brief detail the organization of the work of these two all-important functional offices of the French Foreign Ministry.

The office of economic, financial, and technical affairs is divided into two main sections: one, economic and financial and, the other, technical accords. The first consists of three divisions, each having to do with a group of related affairs, as follows:

a) International economic organizations; Economic and Social Council of the United Nations; general economic policy; raw materials; economic and financial negotiations with the United States, Great Britain, Ireland, and Egypt; economic and financial negotiations concerning the French Union; and economic and financial relations with Syria and the Lebanon.

b) Economic and financial negotiations with the countries of Western Europe (except Great Britain), and the countries of Asia and Latin America.

c) Economic and financial questions concerning Germany and Austria; economic and financial negotiations with the countries of Central and Eastern Europe; economic and financial provisions of the peace treaties; the expansion of the commercial attaché service abroad; transfer of funds and budgetary matters.

The technical accords section is divided into two divisions concerned with:

a) Studies and negotiations regarding the protection of French economic interests abroad, as well as in France; the liquidation of German assets abroad.

b) Studies and negotiations concerning international transport, including civil aviation, shipping. railways, river navigation, and road transport.

The five sections into which the office of economic, financial, and technical affairs is divided, correspond roughly to the three Offices among which work concerned with economic and financial affairs in the Department of State is distributed. Under Secretary William L. Clayton, heading the general economic and financial work of the State Department, was in 1946 the counterpart of M. Herve Alphand, Inspector of Finance, and Director General of Economic, Financial, and Technical Affairs in the French Foreign Ministry.

Similarly, the four sections into which the work of the Office of Political Affairs in the French Ministry is separated correspond to the four Offices of European, Far Eastern, Near Eastern and African, and American Affairs in the Department of State. In the French Ministry the sections are: a) Europe; b) Asia and Oceania; c) Africa-Levant; and, d) America.

In 1946 the Director General of Political Affairs in the French Foreign Ministry, M. Couve de Murville, combined the functions in the Department of State of Assistant Secretaries James C. Dunn, with supervision over the Offices of European, Far Eastern, and Near Eastern and African Affairs, and Assistant Secretary Spruille C. Braden, with supervision over the Office of American Affairs.

In the Department of State the Office of European Affairs is divided into six Divisions, namely, British Commonwealth, Eastern European, Central European, Southern European, Northern European, and Western European Affairs. In the French Foreign Ministry the European Section comprises only four, namely, Western Europe, Central Europe, Southern Europe, and Eastern Europe. In the Department of State the Office of European Affairs is headed by a Foreign Service Officer with the rank of counselor of embassy; in the French Ministry the European section is likewise headed by a counselor of embassy. The four division chiefs in the French Ministry are all counselors of embassy; in Washington two of the division chiefs in the Office of European Affairs are departmental officers of the home service, while the remaining four are Foreign Service officers with the rank of first or second secretary.

The situation reflected by such a detailed comparison of the composition of the European section of the French Foreign Office with the Office of European Affairs of the State Department is sufficiently typical to make unnecessary a similarly detailed comparison of all the other French political sections with their American counterparts. It will suffice to state that while the Office of Far Eastern Affairs in the State Department is headed by a counselor of embassy, the French section of Asia and Oceania is in charge of a French minister plenipotentiary. This section is divided into a Pacific and a Central Asian Division. The Pacific Division embraces the work of the Chinese, Japanese, Southwest Pacific, and Philippine Affairs Divisions into which the Office of Far Eastern Affairs of the State Department is divided. The Central Asian Division corresponds to the Middle Eastern Division of the American Office of Near Eastern and African Affairs.

It is in a comparison of the work of the Africa-Levant section of the French Ministry with the American Office of Near Eastern and African Affairs that the chief differences appear between the organization of the political work of the French Ministry of Foreign Affairs and that of the State Department.

The work of the four sections of political affairs in the French Ministry has been described in a bulletin published in 1946 by the French Foreign Ministry on its central administration as concerned with "correspondence, political work, and centralization of information regarding the general and political policies" of the countries with which the four sections respectively deal, as well as "questions of national defense and public international law having to do with those countries: together with all questions of an economic, legal, administrative, and cultural character, in their political aspect, in concert with the interested technical services" of the Ministry. Finally, the four sections have political responsibility for the military, naval, and air attaché services in their area.*

In addition to the above described functions, the Africa-Levant section in the French Ministry has the special task of overseeing the political, economic, and administrative direction of the French Protectorates of Morocco and Tunisia. This section, headed by a consul general, acting as director, has two principal subdirectors and a chief of bureau as assistants. These officers are all from the French Foreign Service who have had extensive practical experience in the areas under their immediate jurisdiction. The first deputy director in charge of Tunisia, Morocco, and Libya, has assisting him two Division chiefs, in charge, respectively, of Morocco and Tunisia. The second deputy director is charged with affairs in Egypt, Turkey, Syria, Lebanon, Palestine, Transjordan, Iraq, Saudi Arabia and the Yemen, corresponding to the Division of Near Eastern Affairs in the State Department. A third division, known as the African Bureau, with jurisdiction over Ethiopia, Liberia, the Union of South Africa, and European possessions in Africa, corresponds to the African Division of the Department of State.

FRENCH FOREIGN OFFICE PROCEDURE

The procedure of the French Ministry of Foreign Affairs in the handling of correspondence is on a considerably simplified and less extended scale than that of either the State Department or the British Foreign Office. This is to a certain extent a consequence of the fact that in the French Foreign Ministry authority is less widely diffused, with less necessity for the wide dissemination of correspondence.

The Secretariat of the Ministry, directed by a minister plenipotentiary of the French career Foreign Service, receives and dispatches all correspondence. A report received by mail from French diplomatic and consular representatives abroad is known as a *depeche,* while other correspondence, received from private individuals or from other French Government services, are known as letters. Those received from the field are in an original and two

* Administration Centrale, Ministère des Affairs Etrangères, Paris, Imprimerie Nationale, 1946.

copies. Upon receipt they are registered according to number, date, and with a brief account of their subject matter. The original is given a symbol marking with a green pencil indicating to which of the twenty-four principal sections of the Foreign Ministry it is to be forwarded for consideration and possible action.* The office of the Ministry for Foreign Affairs is indicated by the symbol CM; that of the Secretary General, SGL; the Director General of Political Affairs, DGP; the Africa-Levant section, AL. If a section of the Ministry other than that to which the original is routed is likely to be interested in the communication, the original is stamped "copy communicated to" with the addition of the section's symbol. The copy is stamped "original sent to" followed by the symbol of the section to which the original has been sent. In the event that the communication is of interest to more than three sections a *Fiche de Circulation* (routing slip) is made up on forms printed for that purpose giving in concise and brief form the number, date, and subject matter of the communication, with its origin, and where the original has been routed. This form is sent to other possibly interested sections which may call for the original in case it is desired to be seen. In such circumstances the original document would bear also a notation, *Fiche de Circulation Envoyee à* —followed by the symbols of the sections to which one or more such notices had been sent.

After registration the *depeches* and letters are deposited in trays marked with the symbols of the various sections of the Ministry. Twice daily, in the morning and afternoon, messengers place the contents of the trays in small hand satchels bearing the symbols of the sections for which the papers are intended and these are delivered by hand. Telegrams received, in contrast with the Department of State where copies are mimeographed and given wide distribution, are made in only one or two copies in order the better to preserve their security.

* Of these twenty-four principal sections only twenty have full-fledged registry offices known as "bureau d'ordre." Four, namely, those of the Secretary General, and those of the Directors General of Political, Economic and Administrative Affairs have only a restricted registration system. As explained to me in the Ministry, if these sections undertook to register all papers passing into their possession their registry offices would assume the form of the central registry office maintained by the Secretariat.

Outgoing instructions and letters are registered by the Secretariat in a manner similar to incoming communications. These are prepared in an original and single copy and the copy is returned to the section preparing the communication where it is given its index number and filed.* Incoming communications similarly are given index numbers not by the Secretariat but by the different sections to which the originals are sent and these are retained eventually in the separate files of the respective sections. At the end of four or five years the old files of the various sections are forwarded to the central archives in the Ministry. This system, involving an initial decentralization of files of current business, is in conformity with the British rather than the American practice. The great disadvantage of the French system is that a section desirous of obtaining access to a paper not in its own files must first address itself to the Secretariat to learn to which section it was originally routed and then to the section in question.

The most striking difference between the procedure of the French Foreign Ministry in the handling of correspondence and the American and British procedures is in the original reference of such correspondence. Whereas in the State Department and the British Foreign Office incoming despatches and letters are routed initially to the lowest echelons in the hierarchy of officers charged with acting on correspondence, in the French Foreign Ministry despatches and letters are routed initially to the highest echelons and filter down rather than up the scale.

As has been seen, a despatch received from the field in the Department of State or in the British Foreign Office, unless of an extraordinarily important character, goes first to the junior officer dealing with the country with which the communication deals. It then makes its way, depending upon its importance, up the scale of officers through an assistant chief of a division, the chief of the division, the deputy director of an office, the director of an office, an Assistant Secretary, an Under Secretary and, in exceptional cases, to the Secretary of State himself.

In the French Foreign Ministry the process is precisely the re-

* The file number is not given until action on it is completed and it is ready to be filed. The blank spaces of the file numbers in the registration books, accordingly, afford a check on the dossiers which are in current use.

verse. Incoming communications are routed initially to the Directors General (corresponding to the Assistant Secretaries of State in the Department of State) or, to the directors of sections who make the decision themselves as to whether the matter is of sufficient importance to claim their personal attention or should be delegated to subordinates. This delegation may take the form of a written directive endorsed in the margin of the paper or may be oral. In this respect the French system differs markedly from the definite and businesslike precision with which papers are dealt with in the British Foreign Office. The system of the Department of State, while less rigid than the British, would seem to be less informal in character than that employed in the French Ministry.

A French official in explaining the French procedure, expressed the view that the French system of placing the initial responsibility for action on the higher echelon of officials in the Ministry rather than on the lower was in keeping with French national character. This centralization rather than diffusion of authority makes of course for great delay in dealing with correspondence.* It provides the answer to the very obvious question arising in the mind of anyone acquainted with the working of the Department of State as to how the French Ministry functions on the basis of so limited a distribution of copies of despatches, letters, and telegrams received by it. An incoming despatch or telegram which would be given a distribution of fifteen or twenty copies in the Department of State would receive in the French Ministry of Foreign Affairs a distribution of not more than three or four copies. In the State Department officers tend in consequence to be overwhelmed by the amount of reading which they must undertake, oftentimes of communications of but very indirect interest to their work. In the French Ministry officers, particularly those of junior rank, appear to work sometimes without that broader knowledge of current affairs relating to their work which is enjoyed by their American colleagues.

* When inquiry was made whether a correspondence requiring urgent action did not suffer by this system it was explained that junior officers made a practice of examining periodically the trays of papers in the offices of the chiefs of sections and thus exercised an informal surveillance over correspondence for its prompt dispatch.

RECRUITMENT AND TRAINING
OF FRENCH PERSONNEL

In Great Britain the revolutionary step has been taken of amalgamating the British diplomatic, commercial, and consular services, together with the home service of the Foreign Office, into a single Foreign Service. This was a sufficiently bold advance in itself, reflecting recognition of the need of a drastic overhauling of the British Foreign Service to bring it in keeping with the new responsibilities with which it is faced.

In France the French Government has adopted an even more drastic and sweeping measure in the effort to give the French Foreign Service and the whole civil service apparatus of the government a new life and growth. In 1945 the Government took the unprecedented measure of placing on a common basis the recruitment and training of all their civil services, including the Foreign Service of the Ministry of Foreign Affairs, as well as the other civil administrations.

Formerly candidates for the French Foreign Service were subject to examinations given by the French Ministry of Foreign Affairs. These were in three successive stages combining both oral and written tests, the first in modern languages, the second before a commission presided over by a minister plenipotentiary, and the third before a commission headed by an ambassador. Applicants, who were weeded out at each successive stage, had their choice of two distinct tests, one known as the *grand concours* and the other, the *petit concours*. The first, the severer test of the two, led to appointment as attaché of embassy or deputy consul, the successful aspirant being assured of more rapid advancement in the service. Candidates who elected to choose the simpler form of examination by reason of their more limited qualifications began their careers as vice-consuls, if successful, and proceeded in slower stages through the consular service, with the possibility always afforded them, however, of rising to the rank of minister. Candidates for service in the Ministry of Finance or the Ministries of Interior or Agriculture were recruited separately by those ministries. Training for the French civil service was offered not by a public but by a private institution in Paris known as the *École Libre des Sciences*

Politiques, organized by a group of French thinkers aroused after the French defeat of 1871 by the need of a drastic reform of the State machinery, which since its establishment had enjoyed a virtual monopoly in training French diplomats, officers, councilors of state and other aspirants to senior posts in the French Civil Service.

The parallel between 1871 and 1940 leaps to the eye. The French State apparatus when faced by the greatest test which had confronted it in modern French history was found suspended in a vacuum, unresponsive to the will and desires of the French people and incapable of functioning effectively with the exception of a few outstandingly efficient services of which the French Foreign Service was the most conspicuous example. It was in full recognition of the failure generally of the French civil service to meet the test with which it was faced in 1940 that the Provisional Government in 1945 undertook so completely to transform the recruitment and training for the public service.* It must be said in justice to those French Foreign Service officers with whom I came in contact during the war that, with one or two notable exceptions, they distinguished themselves by sabotaging by such means as were available to them the collaborationist direction of the Vichy Government and by close co-operation with the Allies at great personal risk. Stationed as I was during the war at Tangier I had personal evidence of these activities of my French colleagues under most trying conditions. The entire personnel of the French Consulate General was recalled to Vichy in the summer of 1942 under German pressure by reason of its friendliness to the Allies. Yet the new personnel of the French Consulate General sent from Vichy showed itself no less friendly than their predecessors.

Many of the officers who served under Vichy after the Armistice did so only with the greatest reluctance. One officer, an old friend, Claude Clarac, serving as Consul in Tetuan, used to come weekly to our Legation in Tangier to announce to me that he had decided he could not stick it out longer but that he felt compelled to resign and to join the forces of General de Gaulle in London. I had to

---

* Cf. Texts Relatifs à la Reforme de la Fonction Publique published in Supplement No. 397 of the *Journal Officiel* and containing Extraits du Journal Officiel des 10 et 19 Octobre 1945.

explain to him many times that the assistance he was rendering his country and the Allied cause by the information he was able to furnish me from Tetuan was of far greater importance than any aid he might hope to render in London. Men who stuck it out like Clarac and whose actions in continuing to serve Vichy were misinterpreted and misunderstood were in many cases greater heroes than those who rushed to identify themselves with the Allies. This is an appropriate time as any other to pay tribute to the French colleagues whom I worked with under the circumstances I have indicated during the war. They included Jacques Meyrier, now French ambassador to China; Claude Clarac, now counselor of embassy in Indo-China; Triat, at present French consul general in Liverpool; Roger Chambon, French consul general in Boston, with a glorious resistance record; Lavastre, now in the service of the French Government in Germany; Charpentier, counselor in Moscow; and Juge de Montespieu. Whatever one may have said of them for serving under Vichy, I can say of them from personal experience that in their own separate way they served the cause of freedom well.

The French Foreign Service was not of course without its collaborators with the enemy: those men who hated Hitler less than the advocates of social reform in France, such as Leon Blum. Such men were generally to be found among the tired older ranks attracted to Pétain and the so-called National Revolution by a desire for security.

The purge of these men and the losses suffered by the French Foreign Service through its officers at the front, necessitated as early as 1944 a preliminary reorganization to bring into the Service additional personnel. Under a decree (April 26, 1944) of the French Committee of National Liberation, provision was made for an auxiliary corps of officers to be admitted on probation for a period of three years. Frenchmen who had taken an active part in the resistance movement were given preference and some one hundred were admitted under these circumstances, approximately fifteen as counselors or consuls general, thirty-five as secretaries of embassy or consuls and the remainder in a more junior capacity. In order to be integrated into the French Foreign Service on a permanent career basis such auxiliary officers must pass an appropriate examination in 1947 and they are, of course, subject to dismissal previously if they have failed to demonstrate suitable capacity.

A more fundamental reorganization of the French Foreign Service was undertaken, as has been mentioned, in 1945 as a part of a general reform of the whole of the French civil service.

The measures taken by the Government to that end offer in their introduction an explanation of the reasons actuating this notable reform. The French public services, it is stated, have not kept pace with the times. Sufficient account has not been taken either of the economic and social consequences of the industrial revolution of the last century or of the need for the democratization of the State. The necessary recasting of the French administrative machine involves a whole diversity of problems complicated by the varied character of the personnel in the service of the State, ranging from judges, diplomats, and public administrators to technicians and officers in the colonial service. While recognizing the necessity of treating separately these different categories, the authors of the reform proclaim that priority is due the general problem of the training and recruitment of the higher echelons of civil servants for the Council of State, the civil services of the ministries, the Foreign Service, the corps of inspection and control, and the prefectoral corps.

With such a purpose in view the reform provides for the establishment at the Universities of Paris and Strasbourg and eventually at other universities, Institutes of Political Studies having as their mission the imparting to students, whether or not destined for the public service, general political and administrative training. With a view to throwing the civil service open to all classes of the population, the State undertakes to provide for the expenses of those students applying for admission who are unable to meet the expenses of tuition.

The Institutes are intended to become in time feeders of trained students aspiring to a public career. Those destined for the higher civil service ranks, including the career Foreign Service, will pass into the newly established National School of Administration which will be open likewise to those who have demonstrated

[237]

previously by five years of practical experience in State administrative posts their fitness for higher responsibilities.

While the Institutes of Political Studies will train candidates for appointment both as executives and administrative technicians, known respectively as civil administrators and administrative secretaries, only those aspiring to nomination in the first mentioned category, who will comprise higher officials dealing with policy matters, will be eligible for admittance to the National School of Administration. Candidates for the school, who will be admitted on probation, will receive an initial allowance of 54,000 francs the first year (approximately $450) rising to 75,000 francs the third and final year ($625).

Admittance to the school will be open through competitive examination each year between September 15 and November 15 to candidates of French nationality, including women. If admitted after having been employed five years in the French civil service they must be at least twenty-six and not more than thirty on the January 1st preceding. All other candidates must not be more than twenty-six years of age and with certain specified exceptions, must possess a recognized diploma. Successful graduates must undertake, against heavy financial penalties, to remain in the government service for at least twelve years and those refusing to accept the obligation are required to reimburse the State for the salaries received by them while attending the school.

The written examinations held in 1945 for admission to the school included the writing in six hours of a composition on the influence exerted by the principles of 1789 upon world political evolution, and whether the application of these same principles fully suffices, from an economic and social point of view, to meet the needs of man in modern society. The examinations provided also for a second composition to be completed within a period of three and a half hours. The candidate chose one of the following subjects: international consequences of the discovery of the atomic bomb, the rule of unanimity in the Councils of the Great Powers, the Arab problem, respective advantages and disadvantages of proportional representation in electoral matters, woman suffrage and its consequences, parliamentary and presidential government, difficulties of reconstruction in France, whether and by what means the demographic curve of a country may be modified, and the future of French agriculture.

Having passed successfully the foregoing tests the candidate is qualified to take the oral examinations comprising an interrogation during fifteen minutes on a subject relating to the section of the school to which he is seeking admission. In the case of the foreign affairs section the subjects are taken from diplomatic history since the Treaties of Westphalia, and from general economic geography. In addition, the candidate is required to comment on some text of a general character, followed by a conversation with the examining board having to do with the interpretation of the text. There are, further, two oral interrogations on subjects left to the choice of the candidate.

The school is divided into four sections: (1) general administration; (2) economic and financial administration; (3) social administration; and (4) foreign affairs, the last preparing for appointment in the service of the Council of State, and as attaché of embassy, duty consul, and deputy commercial attaché, third class.

Upon registering for admission the candidate is expected to indicate the section of the school which he desires to enter. While due consideration will be given the preference expressed he may be shifted, during the period of three years' instruction, to a different section from that elected in accordance with the decision of the school authorities. Accordingly a candidate aspiring to a Foreign Service career, even after he has passed the searching examinations to which candidates for the civil service are subject, has no assurance today in France of realizing his aspirations. He may instead be offered an appointment in the Ministry of Finance or the Interior. This is found particularly galling by members of the old conservative families in France who for many years looked upon service in the French Foreign Ministry as a prescriptive right accruing to them by virtue of their titles or background. The members of the French Provisional Government, most of whom have been bred in a different school and have their eyes faced toward the future rather than the past, look anything but favorably these days upon prescriptive rights.

During the first year of the school the successful candidates are assigned, for practical acquaintance with current governing problems, to administrative services in the French provinces, to French North Africa, or abroad in the French Foreign Service. With a view to enlarging to the greatest possible extent the perspective of the probationers, those who have been admitted from specialized public services are assigned to administrations having the most general tasks, such as the Prefectures, or they may be assigned to university towns to complete their general culture, or sent to French Morocco to work with French civil administrators, the pivots of French administration there. Upon the completion of this first year of practical experience they are required to submit a thesis on the work accomplished by them. Those who pass satisfactorily this further test will be permitted to continue in the school for a two years course of academic work.

The courses and lectures are under the direction of professors drawn from the principal French universities as well as specialists in the different French ministries and administrative agencies. Certain lectures on the broad problems of contemporary national and international life are attended by all the students of the school, irrespective of the particular sections to which they may be assigned, while others of a more technical character are reserved for the students of particular sections. While undergoing their courses of instruction students are assigned successively to several ministries or other government agencies under the direction of an active civil servant for their training. They are not assigned uniquely for the despatch of current business nor may they remain more than eight consecutive months in the same administrative service.

Upon the completion of the three years, students will undergo special examinations for each of their respective sections. They may exercise their choice in the order of their grades for the posts open in the different administrations for which their sections have prepared them. The board of examiners will comprise in the case of those in the section of foreign affairs, four persons chosen by reason of their general competence in the four sections of the school, two or more civil servants representing the Ministry of Foreign Affairs, and one or more language examiners.

These examinations are expected to conform in their general character with the examinations given by the French Ministry of Foreign Affairs to candidates for the Foreign Service career. In

1945 such examinations combined the short-answer form of examinations for the American Foreign Service with the essay type of examination on which principal emphasis had previously been placed under the French examining system.

As a further stage beyond the National School of Administration, the reform of the French civil service provides for the establishment of a Center of Higher Administrative Studies under the direction of that school. The center is intended to broaden the usefulness of persons who have spent at least six years in government service, and to equip adequately for their new tasks those qualified individuals in private employment who desire to transfer to the service of the State. The center will concentrate its attention upon three principal fields of study; administrative problems of metropolitan France, those of overseas France, and the management of nationalized enterprises.

The French civil service reform strikes not alone at methods of training and recruitment but it involves as well a thorough reorganization of the classification and advancement of existing personnel. While formerly each ministry recruited and promoted its staff according to variable standards, the new legislation provides for a uniformity in classification and advancement such as exists under our own federal civil service. Comparable also in some degree to the British classification of Foreign Service personnel into Branches A and B, the French reform establishes two categories, the one of Civil Administrators, and the other of Administrative Secretaries into which the whole of the French civil service, including the Foreign Service, will be classified. The first, corresponding to British Branch A, will provide career French Foreign Service personnel and the executive personnel generally of the French administration concerned with the important functions of planning, co-ordination, and questions of policy. The second category, corresponding to British Branch B, will provide the administrative technicians.

In order to adapt the French Foreign Service to the new scheme of organization providing for the creation of five classes of civil administrators, the French Ministry of Foreign Affairs has drafted legislation providing for the special classification of its own personnel into five categories, namely: (1) administrators of foreign affairs; (2) specialists for the Eastern and Far Eastern services; (3) administrative secretaries of foreign affairs; (4) temporary corps of certain senior officers (including accounting, cultural relations and administrative officers of the Ministry); and (5) officials of specialized services (including code clerks, archivists, translators, and couriers). Officers will pass their entire careers in these categories with the single exception that those in the third category will have the possibility, after at least ten and not more than fifteen years of service, of being promoted to Administrators of Class II or III.

The career personnel of the French Foreign Service falls within the first category of administrators and, under the Foreign Ministry's proposals, would be divided into five main classes, exclusive of two classes of ministers plenipotentiary. The following table shows this proposed classification, with the rates of base pay and number of years necessary to be spent in any one of the classes or grades before promotion to the next highest:

Class	Salary (in francs)	Years of service necessary for promotion
Minister, Class I		
Minister, Class II		2
1. Senior Administrator	300,000	2
2. Administrator, Class I:		8
Echelon 4	270,000	
" 3	255,000	
" 2	240,000	
" 1	225,000	
3. Administrator, Class II:		4
Echelon 4	210,000	
" 3	195,000	
" 2	180,000	
" 1	165,000	
4. Administrator, Class III:		6
Echelon 3	150,000	
" 2	135,000	
" 1	120,000	
5. Deputy Administrator	105,000	1

The foregoing amounts represent the proposed base pay of French Foreign Service which are subject to income tax and to a retirement deduction. They receive in addition a cost-of-living allowance and an allowance based on the number of children in the family. These two allowances are subject to a further augmentation to bring them into adjustment with the loss sustained by the depreciation of the franc in different countries.

The cost-of-living allowance of an ambassador is at the rate of 304,000 francs annually, that of ministers plenipotentiary, Class I, 228,000 francs, and of ministers plenipotentiary, Class II, 190,000 francs. The computation of the cost-of-living allowance of other officers of the French Foreign Service is effected according to scales established for four zones into which French Foreign Service posts abroad are classified. For an officer in charge of a consulate general, the cost-of-living allowance ranges from a minimum of 266,-000 francs in Zone One to 920,000 francs in Zone Four; for an officer in charge of a consulate, from 180,000 francs to 620,000 francs. A minister plenipotentiary not serving as chief of mission, or a counselor of embassy, receives a cost-of-living allowance ranging from 220,000 to 800,000 francs. A secretary of embassy, 120,000 to 450,000. For the first child, the cost-of-living allowance is increased by 15 per cent, for the second by 12 per cent, for the third by 10 per cent and for each additional minor child by 8 per cent. On the other hand, French Foreign Service officers who are unmarried suffer a diminution of their cost-of-living allowance by 20 per cent.

Representation allowances are granted in the French Foreign Service only to chiefs of mission. The highest amount is granted the French ambassador in London with a total of 2,265,000 francs, followed by Moscow with 2,253,000 francs, Washington 2,106,000 francs, Brussels 1,632,000 francs, Ankara 1,600,000 francs, Belgrade 1,512,000 francs, Ottawa 1,000,000 francs, and falling to an amount of 297,000 francs in the case of the French ambassador at Lima. The French minister at Copenhagen receives a representation allowance of 1,310,000 francs, that at Sofia 1,086,000 francs; allowances fall as low as 141,000 francs received by the French minister to Haiti.

The French Foreign Service officer, passing from the National

School of Administration, would begin his career as vice-consul, attaché of embassy, assistant commercial attaché, or assistant press attaché within the category of deputy administrator. Upon reaching the third echelon of administrator, Class III, he would be eligible for appointment as secretary of embassy, consul, commercial attaché or press attaché, and upon promotion to a similar echelon of administrator, Class II, he would be eligible for assignment as counselor of embassy, consul general, or commercial counselor.

Ministers plenipotentiary of Class I would be chosen exclusively from members of Class II, with at least two years of service, while those of Class II would be chosen, without particular conditions of seniority from administrators of Class I, as well as from civil administrators in other ministries of the government with at least fifteen years of public service and under the condition that the number of these last will not exceed 10 per cent of ministers plenipotentiary of both classes.

In reorganizing the French Foreign Service, the French Ministry has studied carefully the British reorganization introduced in 1943 as well as the stopgap American legislation of 1945. The French Government has been particularly impressed by the decision taken on the part of both the American and British Governments to consolidate under the aegis of the Foreign Service those government civil agencies functioning abroad on behalf of other departments. To that end the new legislation brings under the supervision of the Ministry of Foreign Affairs the commercial attaché service, formerly directed by the Ministry of National Economy, and that of the press attachés directed previously by the Ministry of Information.

It will be seen that the reforms undertaken by the French Government for the improvement of the French civil service, including the Foreign Service, go beyond anything known to be projected by other governments. They are a measure of the profound French dissatisfaction with the irresoluteness and incapacity of the French State apparatus as a whole before the crisis which confronted it in 1940 as well as earlier. As in the case of most government reforms, the innovations appear most attractive—on paper. The manner of their application, however, can alone ultimately determine their real merit and this will not be apparent for some years. In any case the reforms are interesting, if for nothing else, by reason of the evidence they give that France to a greater extent than Great Britain has recognized the need of a complete refurbishing of its Foreign Service, along with its civil service as a whole, to adapt it to the unprecedented problems of the modern world. Great Britain's triumphant survival of the test of 1940 has made such wholesale reform less imperative than it is to France. Yet both in Great Britain as well as in the United States there is happily a healthy widespread consciousness of the need for a searching inventory of existing administrative processes to make them more adaptable to new conditions. So far as the Foreign Service is concerned, the French reforms have the great merit of bringing the future French Foreign Service officer, during the period of his instruction in the National School of Administration, into intimate contact not alone with the particular work and problems of the Ministry of Foreign Affairs but also with those of other ministries, thus providing him with a greatly extended background and increasing his effectiveness as a French representative abroad.

APPENDIX C

HONORS AND COMPARATIVE RANKS OF FOREIGN SERVICE OFFICERS

THE UNITED STATES Navy Regulations prescribe that upon an official visit to a United States naval vessel by Foreign Service officers the following gun salutes shall be accorded them: an ambassador, 19 guns; a minister plenipotentiary, 15; a minister resident or diplomatic agent, 13; a chargé d'affaires, 11; a consul general, 11; a consul, 7; and a vice-consul, 5.

The question of relative precedence between Foreign Service officers abroad and Army and Navy officers has been the subject of much dispute. The chief of mission, whether an ambassador, minister or chargé d'affaires ad interim, as the senior representative of the United States Government, would normally take precedence over any officer of the Army or Navy whatever that officer's rank. During the war the question became of something more than academic interest in connection with the possible capture by the enemy of Foreign Service officers and the treatment to which they might be entitled in relation to military officers. The question of their comparable rank, as suggested by the Department of State, was as follows:

[246]

Foreign Service Officer	*Army Officer*
Ambassador	Full General
Minister (E.E. & M.P.)	Lieutenant General
Minister Resident; Diplomatic Agent	Major General
Counselor, First Secretary, or Consul General	Brigadier General
Second Secretary or Consul	Colonel
Third Secretary or Vice-Consul (of at least the then Class VIII, now Class V)	Major
Third Secretary or Vice-Consul (below former Class VIII, now Class V)	Captain
Foreign Service Clerk commissioned as Vice-Consul	Lieutenant

INDEX

7

Gifts: 188, 208-209
Giraud, General Henri Honoré: 43
Glassford, Admiral William A.: 62
"Golden Age of American Diplomacy": 5, 15
"Good-Neighbor" policy: 49
Government agencies, U. S.: 49-63, 162, 177-179, 188, 195
Government Career Service: 4
Governments, Foreign, assignment to: 178-179
Great Britain: 59, 76, 84, 104, 105, 126, 127, 128
Greenland: 62
Gun Salutes: 246

Hackworth, Green H.: 3*n*
Hague, The: 27
Hamburg: 6
Hammond, Ambassador: 11
Harvard University: 140
Hawkins, Harry C.: 125
Hawthorne, Nathaniel: 6
Hazards, health: *see* Diseases
Health provisions: 23, 30
Health reports: 60
Hectographing: 51
Henry VIII, King: 212
Henry, O.: 8
Hitler, Adolf: 236
Honors, gun salute: 246
Hoover, Herbert C.: 13
Hopkins, Frank S.: 94
Hospitalization: 30, 205
Hotel Crillon: 96
Hotel Ritz: 148
Household equipment: 200-201
Huertgen Forest hero naturalized: 116·
Hull, Cordell: 40
L'Humanité: 103

Iceland: 62
Immigration and emigration: 50, 108-111, 114, 120
Inland Transportation Organization, European Central: 128
Inoculations and vaccinations: 205
Inspectors: 187. *See also* Buildings
Intelligence: 216
Inter-American Affairs, Office of: 146
Interior, Department of the: 14-15
Internal Revenue Code: 210
International organizations, assignment to: 179
International Telegraph Union: 132
International Trade, Office of: 55-56, 134
Interpreters: 24, 29, 195
Invoices: 58, 119
Iraq: 72
Italy: 38-39
Ivory Coast: 129-130

"Jackets": 217-220
Jackson, Andrew: 6
Japan: 59, 62
Jay, John: 2
Jefferson, Thomas: 4-5, 79
Jerusalem: 25
Jewish property: 122
Journalists: 68. *See also* Press Relations
Jusserand, Ambassador Jean: 67
Justice, Department of: 114-115

Kabul: 30
King's Secretary: 213
Knabenshue, Paul: 23

Labor Attachés: 99-106
Labor, Department of: 44, 51